TREATING
PEOPLE WELL

✧ ✧ ✧

THE EXTRAORDINARY POWER
OF CIVILITY AT WORK
AND IN LIFE

LEA BERMAN
and
JEREMY BERNARD

SCRIBNER

New York   London   Toronto   Sydney   New Delhi

Scribner
An Imprint of Simon & Schuster, Inc.
1230 Avenue of the Americas
New York, NY 10020

First Scribner hardcover edition January 2018

SCRIBNER and design are registered trademarks of The Gale Group, Inc.,
used under license by Simon & Schuster, Inc., the publisher of this work.

For information about special discounts for bulk purchases,
please contact Simon & Schuster Special Sales at 1-866-506-1949
or business@simonandschuster.com.

The Simon & Schuster Speakers Bureau can bring authors to your live event.
For more information or to book an event, contact the Simon & Schuster Speakers Bureau
at 1-866-248-3049 or visit our website at www.simonspeakers.com.

Interior design by Erich Hobbing

Manufactured in the United States of America

1   3   5   7   9   10   8   6   4   2

ISBN 978-1-5011-5798-1
ISBN 978-1-5011-5800-1 (ebook)

*Dedicated to the individuals who taught us
the most about treating others well:*

My husband, Wayne Berman.
—Lea Berman

My parents, Loretta and Herschel Bernard.
—Jeremy Bernard

CONTENTS

FOREWORD

I have been fortunate to travel a lot in my life. No matter where I have been or whom I have met, treating everyone with kindness and respect is universally appreciated. *Treating People Well* contains terrific examples of how a little extra effort in anticipating another's needs and expressing gratitude can build and strengthen bonds with friends, family, coworkers, and everyone you meet along the way.

During our eight years living in the White House, President Bush and I worked with three outstanding social secretaries, including Lea Berman. Along with her able staff, Lea planned and executed beautiful events with poise and grace. And her flair for entertaining made each occasion memorable.

In the Obama administration, Jeremy Bernard helped carry on the special tradition of excellent service and attention to detail that has been an integral part of welcoming a visitor to the People's House. I'm pleased that Lea and Jeremy are sharing their life lessons and hard-won wisdom about the advantages of cultivating generosity, patience, and self-restraint.

We all have the power to brighten the lives of others in big and small ways. This book emphasizes why it's good for all of us when we try. Enjoy these stories!

Warmly,
Laura Bush

INTRODUCTION

*The White House Secretary should combine keen
perceptions and sensibilities with the strength of Hercules,
the hide of a rhinoceros, great endurance
and a sense of humor.*
MARY RANDOLPH

We were White House social secretaries for two very different administrations—Lea under George W. and Laura
Bush, and Jeremy under Barack and Michelle Obama—but we
are also good friends. Many people have expressed surprise at our
collaboration on this book. How could two people from such dis-
parate political viewpoints find anything to agree on? Sure, we're
foxhole friends of a sort, having lived through a similar experience.
But we stay connected out of a fundamental belief that we both
want what's best for our country and that we can find a way to get
there by working together rather than against each other.

It's not so easy to keep friends on the other side of the aisle in
Washington, where people's careers and success are often built on
the fortunes of the political party they serve. In Washington, your
politics are your living and your identity. We refuse to assume the
worst about those whose views differ from ours; we accept that

they see the world differently not because they're bad people with specious motives but because they come from another place and have another point of view.

During Lea's tenure as social secretary for the Bushes (2005–2007) and Jeremy's for the Obamas (2011–2015), we planned events, of course, but we also managed expectations, handled last-minute crises, defused awkward moments, introduced people who became friends, kept enemies apart, placated unhappy guests (and coworkers), and took orders from our bosses—and sometimes even from people who were not our bosses. We dealt on a daily basis with an extraordinary array of personalities in a highly pressurized environment. In short, we did what a lot of working people do. The difference was our office address: 1600 Pennsylvania Avenue.

The White House is the storied home of our nation's presidents and the seat of the executive branch of the American government. It is also a very real place, a white-columned neoclassical mansion that is at once an office, a home, and a space for social gatherings, clandestine conversations, and meetings of global consequence. The tectonic plates of American politics rub up against one another every day there. Following the direction set by the president and first lady, the job of the social secretary—the official job title is special assistant to the president and social secretary—is to maintain the civility, grace, and style of the White House's traditions so that the real business of governing a democracy can happen. Our job is to treat people well.

In this book, we share the lessons that made us better at our jobs and, at the same time, happier in our own lives.

At the White House, we became avid observers—constantly reading the mood of a room, on the lookout for anything that seemed off-kilter. It could be minor and easy to fix, like not enough chairs set up in the East Room before a performance, or it could be something serious, like a foreign president's interpreter pushing the State Department interpreter out of her chair to prevent the president from getting his own verbatim translations of a critical conversation. We were like old-fashioned beat cops: nothing was too small or too big to escape our attention.

While we were watching, we were learning, keenly aware of the behaviors that made everything go smoothly and those that led to bad feelings, complications, and disaster. So much of success, however you define it, hangs on how we treat others from all walks of life. We saw examples of this each day. If a senior staff member wanted to be included in a White House reception, the one who called us personally and asked about it politely received a very different response from the one who had her third assistant *inform* us that she would be attending. Insisting on your own importance rarely works. Everyone is important, and everyone deserves to be treated well.

We learned these lessons best from the presidents and first ladies we served. They were unfailingly kind to all of their guests, including those who were their political opponents. In fact, they sometimes worked harder to make their disapproving guests feel welcome than they did their friends because they were seeking common ground. There were countless times when we watched our principals try a series of conversational gambits in search of a safe topic with which to engage a nonsupporter. From talking sports to recalling a favorite film, they applied themselves until they found the magic subject that led to a relaxed, comfortable conversation. But it wasn't only guests whom they approached with consideration. Understanding that their words and actions carried unique emphasis and power, our bosses treated their entire staff, whether it was a member of the cabinet, an advisor, or a housekeeper from the residence, with the utmost respect. They also treated each other well, with bonds that were easy and warm. Their marriages were clearly built on friendship, love, mutual esteem, and shared life goals. We came to know what to expect from them because their reactions were reasonable and dependable.

The Bushes and the Obamas are more similar than you might think. Even when their political opponents were harshly unfair, they took the high road because they understood that each president sets a tone for the nation, and that no matter what challenges they faced, they stood a better chance of surmounting them with steadiness, restraint, and decency. Their abiding respect for the dignity of others—not only as a principle but on a practical day-to-day basis—gave them a certain moral authority and made them presidential in the way that the world expects from an American president. We became accustomed to a very high level of public conduct.

Our daily observations of our bosses and our surroundings changed us, teaching us how to work productively in an environment of committed, deeply political, and ambitious people. We saw the importance of cultivating relationships, building alliances, cajoling coworkers, and charming ill-tempered participants. But even long before we became social secretaries, we had made a conscious effort to be likable after we picked up on how much easier life was when we took the time to build friendships—particularly in the workplace. Having people around whom we could trust and rely on made it possible for all of us to exceed expectations. At the White House, we learned how to use specific tools to develop our sense of competence, lessen anxiety, and curb the pressures that give rise to jealousy and jockeying for power. The more quickly we mastered the principles we're sharing in this book, the greater our ability was to help the first family and the White House staff and to do our jobs successfully.

Part of the reason we came to the same conclusions about

treating people well is that neither of us were classic White House political junkies. We were ordinary people placed in extraordinary jobs, and we developed similar methods for accomplishing our goals as deftly and with as little drama as possible. If this approach could work for us in gridlocked times and in an environment where playing politics is all too literal, we realized they could work in a wide range of work and life situations—because what environment is *not* political in some sense?

JEREMY

San Antonio, Texas, where I was born and raised, seems an unlikely place to grow up learning about liberal democratic politics. My parents met while working on the campaign of Maury Maverick Jr., a cantankerous liberal who fought tirelessly for civil rights while serving in the Texas House of Representatives. I attended TMI (the Episcopal School of Texas), went to Hunter College in New York, and then moved to Los Angeles with brief aspirations of being an actor. While working as a waiter at an upscale restaurant with private dining rooms often used for political gatherings, I met David Mixner. David was friends with Bill Clinton, governor of Arkansas, who had just announced he was running for president. Mixner was part of Clinton's original "kitchen cabinet," and we immediately bonded over our mutual passion for politics; he eventually hired me to work on the campaign, where I learned about political fundraising firsthand. I went on to work on the 1993 Inaugural Committee and was appointed by Clinton to the President's Advisory Committee on the Arts for the John F. Kennedy Center. It wasn't until the Obama administration that I would take full-time positions in an administration, first as the White House liaison to the National Endowment for the Humanities, then as a senior advisor to the US ambassador in France, and finally, two years into the administration, as social secretary in the White House.

LEA

I grew up on a grape farm in Ohio, and after graduating from Miami University, I moved to Washington, DC, drawn like thousands of other young people by the lure of national politics. I answered a classified ad in the *Washington Post* for a job as a research assistant and found myself working at Georgetown University's Center for Strategic and International Studies (CSIS), where I began my real education in event planning and fundraising while going to graduate school for Latin American studies at Georgetown at night and preparing for a career in the Foreign Service. I organized the events around CSIS counselor Henry Kissinger's programs for five years before marriage and motherhood, while running my own event-planning company in Washington. I had a lot of friends in Republican politics—people whom we'd entertained frequently over the years—and after the election in 2000, one of them suggested I talk to Lynne Cheney about being the social secretary and house manager at the vice president's residence. The residence was around the corner from my daughters' school—and they told me it was a part-time job. It was definitely not a part-time position, but it was an incredible opportunity. And so in 2001, I became the social secretary to Vice President Richard Cheney, and later Lynne Cheney's chief of staff. I began working as White House social secretary in George W. Bush's second term.

The White House social secretary has to know more than how to serve a cup of tea to the prince of Wales (no teabags, please) or who outranks whom in the official Order of Precedence. Many technical skills are required for a modern social secretary—for example, calculating how long it will take five thousand people to enter the White House grounds for a state arrival ceremony, where to place the press corps in the East Room so they can get their shots without disturbing the guests, and, increasingly, how to prevent visitors from snapping photos in the family residence and posting them on social media, a challenging new dimension to the job. We also had to recognize problems as they arose. If one entertainer wasn't getting along with another before a performance, we made sure their rehearsals took place at different times. If a friend of the president's showed up at the gate with no appointment and no identification, we hurried down to vouch for that person and bring him or her inside without a fuss. Social secretaries need to know not only who the president's and first lady's friends are, but what the administration's policy initiatives consist of so that every event helps further its goals. And although they can never share it with anyone, social secretaries must be familiar with the gossip surrounding the people who grace the president's table. It's vital to know which guests are implacable enemies and who is said to be intimate with whom to prevent difficult personal histories from disrupting important public occasions.

Originally, social secretaries were responsible only for responding to invitations and planning parties for the president and first lady, but today the White House social secretary coordinates all the events that take place in the White House "mansion" or grounds, with the exception of those occurring in the Oval Office or the White House Press Room. The first social secretary, Isabella Hagner, began working for Edith Roosevelt in 1901 and quickly made her role indispensable. Newspapers of the time refer to Hagner as the "real social ruler at the White House." Among her duties was answering the first lady's mail, which included many requests for the Roosevelt family's discarded clothes and pianos. Hagner also had to manage the gifts that regularly arrived for the Roosevelts, one being a parrot named Loretta.

Since Hagner's reign, first ladies have been employing social secretaries for their knowledge of protocol and society, their tact and discretion, and their ability to say no without giving offense.

We opened this book with a quote from Mary Randolph, Grace Coolidge's social secretary, because the qualities she describes—strength, thick skin, endurance, and humor—continue to be useful in today's White House. With a staff of four or five, Lea and Jeremy both worked around the clock; a twelve-hour day was considered a light one. Most weekdays included multiple events that the president or first lady attended, sometimes together and sometimes on their own. The weekends too were packed with back-to-back activities—T-ball games, movie screenings, and unofficial get-togethers with friends. Jeremy remembers that in his first year, 2011, he was preparing for the Wounded Warrior Project Soldier Ride, the White House Garden Harvest, formal state dinners, and a nonstop procession of championship sports team celebrations, to list only a few. While Lea was in the Bush White House, she planned twenty-four parties in twenty-one days during the holiday season, hosting eleven thousand guests over the course of those hectic three weeks. Every administration celebrates annual occasions like the Easter Egg Roll, the Congressional Picnic, the Combatant Commanders Dinners, the Senate Spouses Luncheon, Cinco de Mayo, the Governors Ball—and that doesn't include affairs for worthy causes like the Thelonious Monk Institute of Jazz or the Special Olympics.

It's a glamorous-sounding job that often *was* glamorous: greeting foreign leaders as they entered the Blue Room after waving to the crowd from the balcony at a state arrival ceremony, escorting Steven Spielberg or Meryl Streep into the Diplomatic Reception Room on the night they became lifetime honorees of the Kennedy Center, or watching giddy, happy friends and family spill into the White House after the Inaugural parade, flags flying and Sousa marches pumping outside.

There were behind-the-scenes moments that we loved, like Stevie Wonder unexpectedly breaking into song as guests were departing an afternoon reception, or world-renowned cellist Yo-Yo Ma slipping into a seat with the Marine Band for an impromptu number with the (delighted) musicians, just moments before Prince Charles and his new bride, the duchess of Cornwall, arrived for dinner. Watching the Obamas' playful interaction before a state dinner while waiting for the guest of honor to arrive at the North Portico was something Jeremy will always remember with fondness. For Lea, it was exhilarating when the Bushes sailed out of a dinner and stopped to say, "That was great tonight!" on their way to the elevator at the end of a formal evening.

We were lucky to witness those things, but it wasn't all "Ruffles and Flourishes," the traditional musical fanfare that greets the arrival of the president. There were many less-than-perfect moments, when guests had overindulged at a holiday party and were sick into a potted plant, or began palming silverware and place card holders from the dinner table when they thought no one was looking. The Congressional Picnic, when members of Congress and their immediate families are invited to the South Lawn for a themed picnic and entertainment, was always one of the most challenging events of the year. The day of the picnic inevitably turns out to be crushingly hot and humid. Members of Congress show up with hundreds more additional friends than they tell us are coming, and then become piqued when the Secret

Service Uniform Division officers don't have their impromptu guests on the list. People swarm the president and first lady for hours before finally departing, perspiring and tipsy, centerpieces tucked under their arms.

Even on normal days, we had to be prepared for anything. One of us watched in mild horror as a US senator arrived at the North Portico for a meeting with the president, opened his car door, took a swig of mouthwash, and spat it out on the White House steps, before stumbling drunkenly up the steps to be escorted inside. Events with runners and athletes were also a challenge; more than a few had to be asked not to sit on the State Dining Room table or throw their long legs over the arm of a rare Madison-era armchair. It was enough to make a White House curator cry.

It could also be difficult to get fun-loving guests to leave after an event. In her memoir, Isabella Hagner wrote of a White House aide "who would walk around through the rooms after one of the big receptions, saying in a semi-audible voice, 'Have they no homes, have they no homes?'"

Of course, coming to the White House is a big deal and people want to squeeze every moment of enjoyment out of it, but when the band stops and the butlers start taking food off the buffet tables, the party's over. There were many times, when we were on the third event of the day and the president and first lady were long gone, that guests lingered while all we wanted to do was to go home and soak our feet. That's when the military social aides deployed a crowd-control maneuver called the chicken walk. They would start at the edges of the room and move inward, their feet turned out like chickens, and slowly edge people toward the door. As soon as one room was empty, staffers would close the doors, and then they'd start in the next room. People were never told to leave; instead, a nonverbal cue—moving a bit too close—made guests realize it was time to go.

The White House may be an awesome and sacred place, but it's also a party venue full of people doing what they do at parties. Dealing with trying situations was part of the brief. Everyone has awkward moments, but what matters is how you handle them, for your own well-being as well as for the people you live and work with. Most of us have bosses, and we care what they think—it doesn't matter if the boss is the president of the country or the manager of the local restaurant. The same is true for family members and friends. How we treat them affects how they treat us in return.

There is one basic rule for how to conduct yourself that fits any interaction, and it's the underlying principle of this book: act as if the entire world is watching, and you cannot fail to do the right thing. Most of us like to think of ourselves as good people, and if we sense that what we're doing is public, we're more likely to behave reasonably. (In fact, through our ever-expanding digital world, more and more people probably *are* watching.) Over time, we become more balanced, calm, and confident, which makes our connections with others stronger and more positive. We came to realize this because so much of our job was to be on display. We were the greeters at events, the ones who tiptoed up before an expectant crowd to show a performer where to stand. When you know people are watching everything you do, you stand a little straighter, smile a little more patiently, and try to anticipate the best possible outcome in any interaction.

Ha! you might be thinking. That certainly doesn't seem to be the lesson we could take from our current political climate. Some people heap disrespect on anyone who dares to oppose them, tap into anger and manipulate it for their own benefit, and don't seem to see anything wrong with that. If bad behavior is contagious—as many studies have shown it is—we're in an epidemic.

So is our White House experience relevant today? We think it is. More than ever before, we need to treat one another with dignity, teach our kids the value of kindness and honesty, and show our willingness to listen and collaborate. What would Lincoln, Reagan, FDR, or Kennedy think about America today? They were effective presidents who understood that government worked through mutual accord. It doesn't mean that they compromised their principles or weren't critical of their opponents; rather, they exercised civility as a way to get things done and move the country forward. There have always been partisan, highly personal attacks in politics—Charles Sumner was nearly fatally beaten by a congressman on the Senate floor in 1852 for opposing slavery—but successful presidents, and those who oppose them, understand that showing respect for each other also shows respect for the Constitution, the institutions of government, and the country.

We tried to have good relationships with everyone we encountered at the White House: the Navy steward at the Mess window, the Secret Service Uniform Division officers posted on the ground floor, the part-time butlers, and the calligraphers. (Yes, the White House still uses calligraphers.) Their friendliness in return was sometimes the one bright spot in a long afternoon. Acting with civility helps each of us take back a little of the ground that's been lost in today's public discourse. Tiny steps—daily activities like saying hello to the bus driver or holding a door for someone—add up to a healthier daily life and a better perspective. These moments make us feel decent. In the same way that each unpleasant exchange we have in the course of a day dampens our mood, every affirming interaction builds up and reinforces a positive sense of self.

It's possible that social skills seem to be disappearing because people think manners are a relic of an earlier time. But they still have a crucial impact on professional and personal success: it's not easy to do well in work and in life without some grasp of people skills. Not everyone is born charming, funny, or easy to get along with; these are learned behaviors. Neither of us was born with the interpersonal skills we use today; we became students of human nature and taught ourselves how to get along more comfortably in the world. It didn't come naturally to us to make the first move and introduce ourselves to strangers, as we had to do at the White House, but we saw how much it put people at ease and made them respond in kind. So we swallowed our nervousness—and now it's second nature. Receiving criticism without taking it too personally was another insecurity that we overcame after seeing how much more productive it was to stay cool and look for a solution rather than an excuse.

This book introduces the twelve practices we see as the cornerstones of the art of treating people well. We illustrate each one through our own interactions at the White House: challenging moments with staff, colleagues, partners, guests, and our bosses, behind the scenes and in the hot lights of public events. We'll show how these techniques can be used to improve situations and relationships. We'll also share times we made a misstep and learned a valuable lesson.

We have listed the twelve practices in a particular order because one skill builds on the other. (It's pretty difficult to tell your boss a joke if you don't have some self-confidence, and you'll want to learn to be a more patient listener before taking on the office jerk.) These methods are helpful for people who hope to work more effectively with their bosses and coworkers, small-business owners seeking to expand their professional networks, men and women in search of lasting friendships and relationships, students headed into college or the workforce for the first time, and parents who worry about their tech-obsessed children's ability to interact with others in face-to-face situations. Warmth, reliability, and honesty motivate people to want to help you, to be your friend, and to make a little extra effort on your behalf—just because, at the end of the day, *they simply like you.* It's not a bad way to live.

We know that being socially adept is not something taught in school, and most of us have to rely on our families and peers to impart these important life lessons. Too many of us miss them altogether, write them off, or don't understand why they have any value at all. But the rules of civility are more than tips on etiquette. By creating a template of how we should behave on the outside, they shape who we are on the inside. The manners we display are a visible manifestation of our sensitivity to others. The ability to treat people well is not determined by background, income, or status. It doesn't matter how rich or famous someone is—material success is not a free pass to go through life treating others poorly.

With these tools, you can reconcile honesty and tact, listening and disagreement, respect and freedom of speech. Calmness, good manners, and kindness make people likable, and likability is the binding agent that makes an organization hum, a business prosper, and turns an acquaintance into a real friend. As Maya Angelou, who read her stirring poem "On the Pulse of Morning" at Bill Clinton's first inauguration, once said, "People will forget what you said, people will forget what you did, but people will never forget how you made them feel."

TREATING
PEOPLE WELL

✦ ✦ ✦

CHAPTER 1

Begin with Confidence

Believe you can and you're halfway there.

THEODORE ROOSEVELT

T he so-called White House high is unique. We've seen more than one hardened military professional wander the State Floor with a tear in his eye. It's affecting to realize that as Americans, we share a common heritage with all the presidents who have lived in this historic place. It's hard to be blasé about a visit to the White House: some people become giddy and others get a lump in their throat. We understood this because we never got over those feelings ourselves—the awe of gazing at the portrait of George Washington in the East Room and imagining Dolley Madison ordering that it be cut out of its frame to protect it from the invading British, or the shiver of anticipation when the Marine Band plays "Hail to the Chief."

The flip side of this is that the White House can be an intimidating place to work, from the rigorous security procedures at the gate each morning to the sense of history that hangs in the air. Thomas Jefferson ate dinner *here* in the Green Room; FDR tracked the course of World War II *there* in the Map Room. Working among the ghosts of past presidents and alongside the ambitious men and women who walk its halls today can make you feel small:

you're in the command center of the country's executive branch, where decisions that affect everyone on the planet are made daily. That would rattle anyone, and on your first day of work, you can't help but wonder if maybe you don't belong there at all.

It's perfectly normal to feel out of your depth at times. Even British Prime Minister Margaret Thatcher, nicknamed the Iron Lady, had the occasional moment of uncertainty. Catherine Fenton, social secretary to President George H. W. and Barbara Bush, remembers Mrs. Thatcher giving stirring remarks after receiving the Medal of Freedom from President Bush at a ceremony in her honor. Upon exiting the East Room, she turned to Cathy and whispered, "Was I all right?"

In moments like these, where you're in a new setting or confronted by a mass of striving professionals, you need to take a deep breath and remember to be confident in yourself even if it's the last thing you feel—especially if it's the last thing. As the saying goes, "You only get one chance to make a good first impression." This is your first lesson in treating people well.

Beginning with confidence can dramatically change your outlook, at work and at home, and help to create the calm capability with which real problems (which emerge less often than we think) can be handled efficiently. A confident person inspires trust—one of the most important components of all strong relationships. This empowering approach can take the form of consciously choosing to treat everyone with whom you cross paths graciously, such as saying good morning to a fellow elevator passenger or complimenting a coworker who has just finished a complicated task.

Now, we don't suggest that you should be overly confident. An insecure person speaking more emphatically than others might think he is being persuasive, but bluster is usually unconvincing. Genuine confidence is earned through experience. The best way to stand out is by exhibiting a quiet confidence wherever you go. Lead the way by setting yourself apart.

THE THREE ELEMENTS OF CONFIDENCE

Three tools helped us become more confident in our daily lives, with each flowing naturally into the next. Maintaining a positive attitude is the first step to feeling confident. Being well prepared for whatever you're about to do comes next. And from there, providing reassurance helps *others* build self-confidence and strengthens your entire team in an upward spiral.

That said, don't expect an overnight conversion; being confident takes time and practice. It's normal to feel anxious when beginning a new undertaking, whether it's the first day of school, becoming a parent, or changing jobs. We're no different; we both had the uneasy feeling that getting our social secretary jobs had been some kind of karmic joke. Neither of us fit the profile of a typical White House social secretary. Past occupants of the position typically came from prominent political families.

Witty, charming, and self-assured, Letitia "Tish" Baldrige, Jacqueline Kennedy's social secretary, was a congressman's daughter who had been Jacqueline's classmate at Miss Porter's and Vassar; Baldrige served in the American embassies in Paris and Rome and later went on to write definitive books on etiquette and style. Bess Abell, from the Johnson administration, was the daughter of the governor of Kentucky. Lucy Breathitt of the Nixon administration later became the first lady of Kentucky herself.

While we both had some political experience, we came from

different backgrounds than previous social secretaries had, and we each had our own obstacles to confidence.

JEREMY

I was a terribly shy kid growing up in San Antonio, Texas. In kindergarten, teachers yelled for me to get off the steps and play with my classmates at recess, which I dreaded the way other kids dreaded the dentist. I spent most of my elementary and middle school afternoons with tutors who specialized in learning disabilities because I had severe dyslexia and teachers often had difficulty understanding what I said when I answered a question. Thankfully, my parents recognized this and made certain that I had the education and training necessary to succeed in school in spite of my learning disabilities. And it turns out that politics played a role in overcoming some of my shyness. The majority of my schoolmates were fairly conservative, whereas I had become enthralled by the political conversations and activism of my parents. My parents met during a campaign, and being involved in politics had become a way of life, so although I was introverted in other areas, I was always willing to jump into a political conversation or debate. But it wasn't until my college years, and eventually dealing with my sexuality, that I felt confident enough to start to break out of the shell I had constructed for myself. The coming-out process allowed me to accept myself and gradually allow others to know who I am, which began to diminish my shyness.

LEA

I grew up on an isolated farm in Ohio and always felt unsure of myself around other children; I was so nervous about going to school that I was sick on the first day of every school year until I was thirteen. I didn't know how to strike up a conversation or make a friend. I feared recess because I didn't know how to play with other kids. My social anxieties mushroomed in high school, and I was miserable everywhere—except in class. I was the nerd who loved school but dreaded the cafeteria at lunchtime. College changed everything for me. I loved the freedom of starting fresh in a new place and indulged my passion for politics and history while developing lifelong friendships. But social anxiety is like a chronic condition: you never cure it; you only learn to manage it.

One of my motivations for taking the social secretary position many years later was to prove to myself that I could finally overcome something I'd considered a lifelong failing. If only we had known that feeling like outsiders when we were kids would help us later in life to be more empathetic toward others. When you've been an outsider, you become highly motivated to reach out and prevent others from having those same feelings of isolation.

We are living proof that confidence is a learnable skill. We started with very little of it! Other fortunate people are born with it, but the truth is that anyone can gain enough self-confidence to get along more easily in the world.

Years later, when the two of us compared notes about our first days at the White House, we laughed when we realized we had had such similar mental images of how it could end: with a brawny Uniform Division guard tossing us out onto Pennsylvania Avenue and wiping his hands, with a hearty, "And *stay* out!"

Everyone has his or her own personal worst-case scenario. We wouldn't be human if we didn't imagine such things, but when that image pops into your head, take a minute, acknowledge it, and then think of it as the thing that's *not* going to happen and push it to the back of your mind. Lea's worst fear was being dressed down by either the president or Laura Bush, because they were always so controlled that it would have taken a real disaster to bring them to a verbal outburst. Jeremy's worst fear was that uninvited guests would get into an event.

Self-doubt in a new situation may be normal, but it's best not to put it on display. Have faith that others see your strengths and skills. You must have done something right to get where you are.

STAY POSITIVE

Confidence radiates outward; it makes people relax and eases tense or awkward moments. Upbeat people are likable and non-threatening, and they tend to make others want to respond in the same good-humored way. And that's not just first-day advice. Exuding optimism and self-confidence is something you should strive for every day. There's a Washington saying that the best staff never bring problems to the president and first lady; rather, they bring them solutions. Our bosses always knew they could trust that our attitude would be enthusiastic and solution-oriented. Beginning a new situation with optimism is the first step to lasting confidence.

JEREMY

I came through the White House gates for my first day of work on a cool March morning, the sun shining brightly above me. I was exuberant, although I couldn't help feeling nervous. What was I getting into? Could I really do the job? The White House

is filled with hyperconfident people armed with agendas, political and personal, and I was worried I wouldn't fit in.

The first item on my schedule was the morning senior staff meeting in the Roosevelt Room in the West Wing, across the hall from the Oval Office. The chief of staff sat in the chair reserved for the president when he attends meetings there. As in the Cabinet Room nearby, the back of that chair is slightly higher, a subtle symbol of power. The most senior advisors sat around the long rectangle table; everyone else stood. The meeting began with Danielle Crutchfield, the director of scheduling, reading through the president's schedule, followed by someone in the Communications Office discussing the talking points and issues of the day. Participants gave briefings or updates as needed. My hands trembled, not so much in fear, but more with an excited awareness of where I was. It was easy to be happy, I thought to myself, when you start your day in the Roosevelt Room at the White House!

Just before the meeting concluded, I was introduced to everyone by the chief of staff, Bill Daley, who asked, "How can I get the gig you just left?" I'd been a senior advisor to the ambassador at the US Embassy in Paris. Working at that embassy was one of the most coveted jobs in the government. I laughed along with everyone else at Daley's question, but I also wondered if I would regret leaving the Paris "gig" for the White House. As it turned out, I never had a moment's doubt.

There had been an unusual amount of press with my appointment as the first male and first openly gay person to hold the post. As people slowly dispersed after the meeting, Gene Sperling, director of the National Economic Council, approached me and said, "Man, who is your PR agent?" I laughed nervously, hoping the press was over and intending to keep a low profile going forward.

After the senior staff meeting, I went to the Situation Room and was buzzed inside. I showed my new White House badge, checked my phone at the door, and walked past a roomful of screens and people monitoring them. I picked up the President's Daily Briefing book, which contains details of the president's activities for the next twenty-four-hour period. My name was on the front page, and I was struck with disbelief. I was really here.

My office windows looked out onto the mansion and South Lawn. Sipping an ice tea in a recyclable cup stamped with the presidential seal, I could see the president's Marine One helicopter landing and taking off, a sensational occurrence at the beginning. (Later, my coworkers and I would become oblivious to it.) The windows in my office were actually doors, which allowed me to step out to the roof of the White House, above the Garden Room. My assistant cautioned me to always call the Secret Service before going out so I didn't get shot.

"Shouldn't there be a warning on the window about that?" I asked in astonishment.

There were back-to-back meetings in which I was bombarded by information about events the Social Office was overseeing. Later that day I felt overwhelmed, but instead of expressing that feeling, I decided to focus on my elation at being there, knowing it was important to have a positive attitude from the beginning. *Act like you belong*, I kept reminding myself. It was important to give my staff the confidence to follow my lead. I knew the last thing they needed was someone who appeared hesitant and out of his depth.

I was helped in this by the fact that from my first day, both the president and the first lady were welcoming. When I walked into the area of the West Wing where the president's assistant sits, she greeted me warmly. Moments later the president emerged from his

office, shook my hand, and asked me to step into the Oval Office, which feels more like a movie set than a real place because it is so bright and pristine. Unfortunately, I don't recall anything about that conversation, but I do remember being immediately put at ease by his affectionate hug and his giving me the sense that I belonged there. We chatted and laughed for a few moments while Pete Souza, the White House photographer, snapped a picture. (Within a week there would be a large White House envelope on my desk with a photograph inside of my first Oval Office visit as social secretary.) I was starting to realize that this was my new normal.

That afternoon, I received an email from a friend in San Antonio, my hometown. He'd sent an AP photo of my assistant and me walking from the West Wing, with the caption "He's on the job." It reemphasized to me the pressure and visibility of this new position; any misstep might be a public embarrassment, not just for me but also for the president and first lady.

As I made the rounds, meeting the staff and learning the floor plan of the White House, I made eye contact with everyone I came across and remained very mindful of my posture—standing up straight makes you look and thus feel more confident. I was conscious to acknowledge each person: the Secret Service agent at his post, a housekeeper, a gardener, a fellow staffer. I greeted them, introducing myself and asking how their day was going. I joked about the Hermès tie I'd bought just a few days earlier at the Paris airport duty-free shop in an attempt to use up the last of my euros. The color stood out, a slightly off-orange shade that invited a few comments—some favorable, some not so much. When Mrs. Obama welcomed me into her office in the East Wing, she said, "Oh my . . . your tie!" I froze, until I realized that Kristina Schake, Mrs. Obama's communications director, had told her about how we had joked about the tie earlier that day.

They all burst out laughing; the first lady gave me a warm hug and welcomed me to "the family."

Hours later, the dinner for combatant commanders, an annual reception for top Pentagon officials and their spouses, began in the Blue Room. All the details had been worked out, so my only job was to greet guests. I recall being in awe at how beautiful this historic room looked, facing out on the South Lawn and beyond to the Washington and Jefferson Memorials. At the end of the evening, I walked with the Obamas from the Blue Room to the elevator that would take them up to their residence. This would become a very familiar practice after an event. I felt like I was walking through history. The graciousness of my new bosses enhanced my confidence and my ability to "act the part."

We all have hidden strengths that we tend to take for granted. I did have one big advantage when I began at the White House: I had worked for the Obamas since the inception of the campaign, in February 2007, when I started a fundraising-consulting firm with several colleagues. Raising money and introducing a then-little-known senator to people in California had allowed me to develop a rapport with the Obamas. They were accustomed to my humor, and I had proven to be a loyal supporter. This was a huge benefit. It was intimidating to be dealing with the president and first lady, but knowing them as "people" prior to the White House made it less so. Reminding myself of this on my first day helped shift my perspective appreciably. I realized that my qualifications for the job were never in doubt—except in my own mind.

Here are some things to remember about sustaining a positive attitude:

Remind yourself of your strengths. In the uncertainty of a new situation, it's easy to get in your own way and focus on what you don't know. Instead, try to remember that you have reasons to be confident. Maybe it's your experience, or maybe it's your great attitude or your willingness to work hard. Think about what you bring to the table that's valuable, and take pride in those qualities.

Engage with the people around you. Ask how someone's day is going; make a joke; wish a colleague a good evening; let others see that you're open and hopeful. You'll be establishing yourself as a person who is pleasant to be around.

Look on the bright side. Set a time—maybe a few hours or a day—when you decide to be in a good mood. Make it a conscious choice so that, when daily life intrudes, and you discover a favorite shirt has a stain or your car won't start, you can focus on the things that are going right. It's a circular process: a good attitude makes it easier to stay positive, and before long it becomes second nature.

JEREMY

When I arrived in the White House, the Social Office had already been through two social secretaries and had weathered a high-profile state dinner security breach. Morale was low. White House staffers work long hours in relatively low-paying, high-stress jobs with constant pressure to perform at the top of their game. In exchange, they have the honor of serving their country in a valuable, career-enhancing opportunity. It is said that the average length of service of a White House staffer is eighteen months. By the time I arrived, some of the staff had worked for almost two years in the presidential campaign before coming to the White House and had reason to be weary.

Yet I couldn't hide my feeling of absolute joy at being there. At one point, a Secret Service agent commented that I was "virtually dancing" as I walked from the West Wing to the mansion. I looked around at my staff, with their serious and apprehensive demeanor, and remarked, "Let's step back and look at where we are. We are working *inside* the White House, we work with the president and first lady on a daily basis, *and* we don't have to make life-or-death decisions. We aren't worrying about invading another country or going to war. I hate to steal from Disneyland, but we should feel like we are at the happiest place on Earth!"

I wanted to remind them of how lucky we were to be there, but it was also my intent to make the office feel more fun. Often I used self-deprecating stories, hoping to convey that I had a sense of humor about things. Other times I would ask colleagues to share funny anecdotes about the Social Office prior to my being there. It helped to emphasize that though our work was important, we shouldn't take ourselves too seriously. It didn't happen right away, but eventually the staff reflected what I'd hoped it would be—a warm, cohesive ensemble—and nothing made me more proud.

GET READY

Finding your self-confidence is an important first step. The next is being prepared for the job at hand.

The White House is actually quite small considering how many people work there. Constructed between 1792 and 1800, the modern White House offers the same amount of entertaining space that John and Abigail Adams enjoyed. The State Dining Room can hold 140 for a seated luncheon or dinner and the East Room up to 200. The East Wing was built in 1942, to cover the underground Presidential Emergency Operations Center, and still manages to (barely) hold the staff of the first lady, the Visitors Office, the Military Office, and Congressional Affairs. The small scale of the surroundings made it all the more important for each of us to figure out how everything and everyone worked.

We couldn't help but notice that our bosses, Michelle Obama and Laura Bush, were always prepared for events, big or small. Mrs. Bush read the "line by lines," the Social Office's detailed descriptions of how each event would unfold, and would have her personal aide call Lea with any questions. Before every event, Mrs. Obama received a briefing from the Social Office with details such as where she was to enter or if there was a teleprompter. She listened patiently and then would focus in on particulars that needed special attention. The first ladies' groundwork extended to their guests. They would find out a bit of background about each one, which meant they could approach each guest in a personal and gracious way. Being prepared is a form of consideration.

LEA

There was no reason for me to be *so* nervous in my first weeks as White House social secretary in 2004. It should have been familiar territory. Like Jeremy, I had a track record. In my case, it was being social secretary to Vice President Cheney and Lynne Cheney's chief of staff. Still, when Laura Bush hired me to be her social secretary in November 2004, the shift from one end of the White House to the other was like landing on an alien planet. The butterflies began each day as I drove onto the White

House grounds and showed my pass at the gate. I was cleared through three successive checkpoints, each time drawing closer to the White House until I was directed to park just outside the East Wing doors. It was a real change from the VP side, where I was one of several thousand staffers working in a building adjacent to the White House. It was an odd thing to be in awe of—a parking place—but it was my first concrete indication of how much things had changed. The parking space, the "Good Morning, Madame Secretary" greeting from the Secret Service agents, the deference of the residence staff: focusing on these small things allowed my confidence to grow.

When you're about to enter into a new job or situation, it's immensely helpful to think about at least one thing over which you have control. A little trick I learned is that dressing well and comfortably gives me one less worry in an unfamiliar environment (both President Obama and Mark Zuckerberg famously feel the same way). I chose a favorite heather green wool suit on that first day of work, which I'd worn to my interview with Mrs. Bush the week before. When I'd arrived in the family residence, one of the first things she'd said to me was, "Oh, I have that same suit!" It turned out that we were on the same page about a lot of things. We liked the same kinds of flowers and foods—she wanted to serve healthy, seasonal meals presented in a natural way rather than tiny portions arranged in towers—and was interested, as I was, in the details of hospitality. From that first meeting, she was friendly and inclusive, and the green suit became sort of a good luck charm for me.

In those first weeks I worked closely with Catherine Fenton, the current social secretary; we were overlapping through the month of December at Laura Bush's suggestion so I could begin to get a grasp of the job while experiencing the intensely hectic

White House Christmas. I was grateful for the guidance. But the presence of two social secretaries in the house was tricky and a little confusing for the rest of the staff. Having a trainee along was the last thing Cathy needed in her final, whirlwind weeks, but she couldn't have been more gracious and patient about it. Her kindness was a lifeline—and an example I'll never forget.

Each day we made the rounds, going into the Usher's Office, the kitchen, and the chocolate shop—a tiny, cold, stainless-steel-covered closet where the pastry chef poured out fresh candies and special desserts and which always had a sweet smell hanging over it, even when no one was working there. I met two people I'd be working with closely: Nancy Clarke, the White House florist, and Gary Walters, the chief usher, both of whom had been there for decades. I peppered them with questions. The chief usher is responsible for the day-to-day operations of the Executive Mansion and the ninety permanent staff who work there. My incessant questions must have been annoying, especially at such a busy time, but I couldn't help myself. I felt driven to understand everything, and luckily, Nancy and Gary loved their work and were happy to explain how things were done.

Cathy found me an empty office in the East Wing and showed me "The Files": more than a thousand folders with details of every White House event of the last four years. I burrowed into the temporary office, where I read every one obsessively. I wrote long lists of questions and itemized the things Mrs. Bush had asked me to see to as part of my new duties, some of which required diplomatic conversations and delicate negotiations with people I'd just met.

At the end of my first day, Cathy appeared with a photograph of the extended Bush clan—more than a hundred people—and said, "You should try to learn the names and faces of everyone in the family. They're a closely knit group and some of them visit a lot, and we must recognize and welcome them as family." It seemed like an impossible task at the time, but it proved to be great advice. Family members did visit regularly, and it was worth the effort to be able to greet them warmly because the Bushes appreciate a thoughtful gesture. If word got around that Barbara Bush or George H. W. Bush were in the building, residence staffers would appear from behind hidden doors and greet them joyfully.

I took the photo home to study, my head full of lists, more questions to ask, and people to seek out the next day. I began keeping a pad and pen on the bedside table to write down any questions that popped into my head during the night. I was energized by what lay ahead and resolved to surround the new job from all sides. Improvise, adapt, and overcome, as the Marines say.

Here are some concrete steps you can take to help you feel confident and ready on the first day—and every day:

Do your homework. Research your new organization before you begin. Try to get a sense of your colleagues and their accomplishments. If you've been hired to handle a particular client or area, come in on the first day with some background knowledge and a few fresh ideas. Once you've arrived, don't be shy about seeking information. The more you learn, the more you can excel. Look for sources of institutional knowledge and ask questions. Most people love to give advice, so you will not only be educating yourself, you'll be creating an ally.

Dress the part. Choose clothes that make you feel well dressed but comfortable and in tune with your surroundings. Pick your outfit the night before. It may seem obsessive, but people who get ready this way don't have to worry about a missing button or a stain on their pants, and it saves time in the morning. It's one less thing to be anxious about; feeling at ease is worth a little extra effort. Notice how others dress, especially your boss, as a guideline for what's acceptable. But remember: being neat and well groomed, however casual your office environment might be, shows poise. (And if you're invited to a party and you don't know what to wear, don't be shy about asking the host. It beats showing up in the wrong attire and feeling foolish.)

See and be seen. Hiding in your office or room does not telegraph self-assurance. Move around in your new environment, find out how things work, and get to know the people you're working or studying or living with. Seek out people who can help you become familiar with your new surroundings, and show your interest in building a relationship with them. Being a dynamic, interested colleague lets others know you're committed to working well together.

REASSURE OTHERS

The life of a first lady is not all motorcades, *Vogue* covers, exotic travel, and entertaining world leaders. Today we expect first ladies to work hard, campaign on their own, take policy positions, and be role models. An endless parade of people waits for them: staff with schedules and questions, friends and acquaintances with favors to ask, reporters seeking interviews, and everyone else who just wants to be in their presence. The first ladies we worked for exuded confidence while leading highly pressured lives, but they also understood the value of instilling confidence in others.

Everyone likes to be told that they're doing a good job. Both Michelle Obama and Laura Bush made their staff feel appreciated, with office luncheons in the family residence, staff birthday parties, visits to local eateries, and group tours of nearby museums. One of Mrs. Obama's most memorable perks for her staff were the retreats to Camp David, where there were team-building sessions and guest speakers in the morning, and the remainder of the day was spent relaxing by the pool, playing golf, hiking, or riding around in golf carts. It was her way of letting people know that their hard work was valued.

LEA

Laura Bush had years of experience with the residence staff, as both first lady and the daughter-in-law of the president; she is also a shrewd observer of human nature. She managed the staff in a quiet and efficient way, establishing clear lines of authority and setting routines that made things run smoothly. In the past, she had approved the menu for every meal served at a White House event. After several weeks on the job, I made a routine visit to Gary Walters's office. As he handed me the menus for the next few weeks, he said, "Mrs. Bush told me this morning that she doesn't need to see the menus anymore. She said you would be approving them from now on." He paused and looked at me appraisingly: "That's never happened in my time here."

The story got around pretty quickly. Mrs. Bush had let it be known, in her own subtle way, that she trusted me. It made the staff take me seriously, and it showed *me* that she appreciated the job I was doing. We didn't know each other very well yet, but her trusting me with the menus made me feel all the more ready to succeed.

Everyone has momentous projects at work—occasions that require massive coordination, preparation, imagination, and luck. For a White House social secretary, a state visit is a rite of passage. There are hundreds of people to be organized and instructed on their roles, from the Secret Service at the gates to the Fife and Drum Corps, the chefs, butlers, florists, flag-waving guests, and military aides. There are usually famous entertainers performing, who may turn up late, nervous, or under the influence of a controlled substance. There are technicians and staffers who can make mistakes (like mispronouncing the name of the country of the visiting head of state) that become the only thing anyone talks about afterward, and VIP guests who sulk when they find they're not sitting at the president's table. Wardrobe malfunctions, forgotten lyrics, dead microphones, massive security, and botched arrival announcements are to be expected. In the midst of all this, having bosses who made us feel we could handle anything did wonders for our ability to do so.

It doesn't have to be a state dinner. Inclusion is a form of reassurance that makes people feel part of something bigger than themselves, even if it's just the weekly staff lunch at a local barbecue joint. It's a powerful yet surprisingly easy thing to do for another person, and an incredibly hurtful thing to withhold. Be the person who makes others feel accepted and welcome; there are few other gestures that will make you feel more confident than an ability to get along with others.

JEREMY

As the new kid on the block, I felt a lot of pressure for my first state dinner, for Germany in early June 2011. I had large poster boards that described where Mrs. Obama would walk and stand at various points. It included a detailed time line from the arrival ceremony to the end of the evening when the president and first lady would escort Chancellor Angela Merkel and her husband, Joachim Sauer, to the limousine on the South Drive just steps from the Rose Garden, where the dinner was to be held. My deputy, who had been there from the start of the administration and understood the mechanics better than I did, was on hand as well in case there were any protocol questions to be answered. I was nervous as I began to present the outline of the day. Mrs. Obama was encouraging. "This is much easier than all the hype they make it to be," she said. "Just follow our lead." As we finished going over everything, she closed by saying, "It's going to be sensational. It'll be fine," with a wink to display her confidence in me and in the staff. Her relaxed demeanor made everything we were facing seem doable, allowing us all to take a deep breath and ease into the event ahead. And the German state dinner *was* a great success.

Here are some guidelines on how to reassure others effectively:

Set the tone. Be the first to be kind, inviting, and magnanimous. If you're leading a project at work, welcome each person individually at a team meeting. Plan what you want to say and anticipate some basic questions or complaints that might arise. And then, as you discuss the way forward, isolate what each of your team members has already contributed to the project and what you still expect them to accomplish. This puts you down the path of earning and keeping the trust and respect of everyone around you.

Speak kindly. This is important to remember outside the office too. If you're the coach and your daughter's soccer team has just been handed their fourth loss in a row, draw attention to their hustle and sportsmanship. If you have a friend who's job hunting and losing heart because she can't seem to get past a first interview anywhere, bolster her flagging confidence by reminding her she hasn't landed on the right thing yet and telling her you have faith that she will find it soon. Just as you take encouragement from the trust others show in you, be generous in reminding people of their good qualities.

FINDING THE BALANCE: CONFIDENCE, NOT ARROGANCE

It's wise not to overlook the value of humility as you strive to be more confident. After all, the most effective leaders emanate self-assurance, not self-importance. General George Patton was known for both his tactical brilliance and his arrogance during World War II. His outbursts against some of his troops, the other Allied commanders, and the Russians were not just impolitic; they made his bosses' jobs harder, and they punished him for it by making him sit out parts of the war, despite his acknowledged capabilities as a commander.

If you never have a moment of doubt, if you never second-guess yourself, if you brush off the concerns of others, you may be a bit *too* confident. False confidence can lead to serious miscalculations.

It's also a form of self-indulgence; it masks insecurities with bravado and attention seeking, creating an addiction to being admired rather than a true understanding of the situation.

President Gerald Ford was known as both a confident and a deeply humble man. When colleagues in Congress flattered him, he was quick to say, "I'm a Ford, not a Lincoln." A few weeks after the Fords moved into the White House, the chief usher, Gary Walters (yes, the same Gary Walters—he served in the White House for nearly forty years), received a call from the president early one Sunday morning. Ford said, "I don't have any hot water." Gary immediately offered to send an engineer, and President Ford replied, "There's no problem. I haven't had hot water in two weeks. I've been going down the hall and using Mrs. Ford's shower." Walters was mortified that the president hadn't had hot water since he'd moved into the White House but impressed by how easily his new boss took it in stride. It's no surprise that Gerald Ford was beloved among the residence staff.

So as much as we encourage self-confidence, it's important not to let the pendulum swing too far in the opposite direction. Arrogance alienates; confidence inspires.

CHAPTER 2

Humor and Charm, the Great Equalizers

✧ ✧ ✧

A sense of humor is part of the art of leadership, of getting along with people, of getting things done.

DWIGHT D. EISENHOWER

Humor makes us relax, opens lines of communication, and draws us together. A well-timed joke can defuse an awkward moment like the popping of a balloon: the entire atmosphere of the conversation changes in an instant, allowing us to hit the reset button. It can be risky to make a joke in a tense situation, but now that you're feeling more self-confident, it's time to turn to this often undervalued communication skill.

Many people consider themselves to be either funny or not—as if they were born that way. This simply isn't true. Yes, some people seem to have humor in their bones. But for others, it's an acquired ability. It takes a little practice, but, like confidence and consistency, it can be learned. We will show you how to develop your sense of humor and make it work for you in high-pressure situations. Humor lets us get away with things we might not otherwise be able to do; think of it as a "Get out of jail free" card.

JEREMY

One afternoon I was escorting comedian Jimmy Fallon around the White House, before a taping for Mrs. Obama's Let's Move! initiative, a program to combat childhood obesity. Fallon was then the host of *Late Night with Jimmy Fallon* on NBC, following Jay Leno's *The Tonight Show*. When we walked into the Diplomatic Reception Room, Fallon looked around at the sparse buffet table—bottled water, apples, and a few snacks, the standard setup for a quick television taping—and said, with feigned disappointment, "Is this *it*?"

"We do a little better for Leno when he's here," I deadpanned.

He looked at me for a moment, then burst out laughing. Needless to say, the taping went well. My quip had eased the tension in the air.

Humor also came in handy when Oprah Winfrey and Gayle King arrived at the residence for a private dinner. Gayle was enjoying her success as an anchor on *CBS This Morning*, while Oprah had ended her television show a few years earlier.

I welcomed Gayle first with a warm hug. I noticed Oprah fixing me with a look, as if to say, "What am I, chopped liver?" so as I leaned in to hug her next, I said, "Well, *Gayle* is on the air every day." They both lit up and laughed.

A little voice inside me asked, *Did I really just do that?* But as I'd walked over, Oprah had called out in her signature style, "JEREMYYY!" which set a high-spirited mood. My job was to make guests relax, feel comfortable, and enjoy their experience fully, no matter how well known they were.

LEAD BY (COMIC) EXAMPLE

Most presidents understand that making fun of themselves is endearing. Barack Obama has a sharp sense of humor and much-lauded comic timing, but he also knew how to ham it up when the situation called for it. Every Thanksgiving when he "pardoned" a turkey while his daughters stood alongside him, he told "dad jokes" as they visibly winced. In his final turkey-pardoning ceremony in 2016 (with his two young nephews standing in for teen-aged Sasha and Malia), Obama promised a "corny-copia of dad jokes," and he delivered. "When somebody at your table tells you that you've been hogging all the side dishes, you can't have any-more," he said, "I hope you respond with a creed that sums up the spirit of the hungry people: *Yes we cran.*"

Ronald Reagan loved to make jokes. According to a classic Washington yarn, he wasn't even afraid to jest with the queen of England. In 1982, while he was on a horseback ride with the queen on the grounds of Windsor Castle, the queen's horse is said to have had a bout of prolonged flatulence. The queen reportedly said, "Oh dear, Mr. President, I'm so sorry!" and Reagan supposedly replied, "Quite all right, Your Majesty. I thought it was the horse."

Jimmy Carter, after leaving office, continued to poke fun at himself: "My esteem in this country has gone up substantially. It is very nice now when people wave at me, they use all their fingers."

Calvin Coolidge, known as Silent Cal, was once seated next to a young woman at a dinner party, who told him that she had a bet she could extract at least three words of conversation from him. "You lose," he replied.

Abraham Lincoln was renowned for his self-deprecating

humor and elaborate story spinning, especially during long meetings with favor seekers. ("Were it not for my little jokes," he once said, "I could not bear the burdens of this office.") He had a favorite story about a time when he was splitting rails and a man carrying a rifle walked up to him and demanded that Lincoln look him directly in the eye. Lincoln stopped his work and obliged the man, who continued to stare silently at him for some minutes. Finally the man told Lincoln that he had promised himself years ago that if he ever met a man uglier than himself, he would shoot him. Lincoln looked at the man's rifle, pulled open his shirt, puffed out his chest, and allegedly exclaimed, "If I am uglier than you are, I don't want to live. Go ahead and shoot."

Humor is subjective and situational: a knee slapper to one person may be considered deeply offensive to someone else. As much as we might enjoy comedians like Amy Schumer and Chris Rock, if we repeated some of their jokes to our bosses, we would not get the enthusiastic response that they get from their fans. Sarcasm too is tricky and can easily backfire, especially online. Dark humor is best reserved for intimate friends and family.

Choose a safe topic to make a jab; universal human foibles, for example, are great fodder for jokes. Sexist, ageist, or racist jokes are not. (Does this really still need to be said? Sadly, yes.) Before you make a joke, ask yourself, "Will this offend the person who is the butt of my joke, or will they laugh in acknowledgment?" If it would hurt their feelings, don't say it; it's as simple as that.

Humor makes us more resilient and adept at managing challenges, and it prevents small disagreements from becoming real conflicts. It can be the first step in healing after failure or a loss. In a difficult meeting in which two work rivals are battling it out, the one who makes jokes and eases the tension shows confidence, optimism, and a winning attitude.

We've found that the best building blocks of humor are keen observations of oneself and others and an understanding of nuance, context, and timing. All of these can be learned.

MAKE FUN OF YOURSELF

Not everyone will warm to you immediately. Maybe someone is waiting to see if you're worthy of her trust, or she's shy, or just doesn't like the way you part your hair. One of the easiest ways to disarm a skeptic or potential competitor is to be self-deprecating. The safest thing to mock in this situation—the only person you're sure you can insult without negative consequences—is yourself. It shows that you know you're human and prone to making mistakes like everyone else—and even better, you're secure enough to laugh about it. When Lea made her frequent rounds at the White House to check on the progress of different events, she would call out to her coworkers, "It's me again! Did you miss me?"

Lyndon Johnson had a larger-than-life personality, but he was also capable of lampooning his shortcomings. His social secretary, Bess Abell, remembers how he "apologized" for an outburst directed at her. In September 1967, President and Mrs. Johnson were hosting a luncheon for 140 people in the State Dining Room in honor of King Constantine and Queen Anne-Marie of Greece. As the entrée was served, Bess, who was standing just outside the dining room, suddenly heard Johnson bellow, "Stop! Put your forks down! Get Bess in here!" She quickly walked in and saw that the guests were frozen in apprehension and all eyes were fixed on Johnson. Standing up at the head table, he turned to Bess and shouted, "The meat is bad! When I cut into it, something funny came out. It smells!"

Bess calmly replied, "Mr. President, the entrée today is tournedos Rossini. What you see inside the meat is foie gras—goose liver. That's also what you smell." President Johnson relaxed and said to the others, "Go ahead and eat it. It's okay," and settled back into his chair as if nothing had happened. Bess slipped from the room, having survived a classic social secretary near-death experience.

A few nights later, Johnson called Bess.

"You remember that meat we had at lunch the other day that I thought was bad?"

"Yes, Mr. President. Don't worry. We'll never serve it again," she quickly assured him.

"It's a good thing you told me what it was, or I would have told nine hundred people at the Waldorf tonight not to eat their dinner because something was wrong with it." And he hung up: Lyndon Johnson's apology, wrapped in a joke.

George W. Bush was often the target of comedians for his malapropisms. He was never bothered by it, though, because he understood the value of a good laugh. The ribbing he received was embraced with affection at the White House; the regular meeting of top national security officials in the Bush White House was even renamed "The Strategery Meeting" after Will Ferrell, as Bush, used the word on *Saturday Night Live*. Terms such as *misunderestimate* and *I'm the decider* became part of the West Wing lexicon. He even beat comedians to the punch by telling many jokes at his own expense. He opened the 2005 Correspondents' Dinner, for example, by saying, "I look forward to these dinners where I'm supposed to be funny . . . intentionally." He always understood that when you make fun of yourself, you take away the power of your detractors.

JEREMY

Soon after President Obama's second inauguration, I met up with him following a taping of "West Wing Week," the weekly web episode produced in the White House Communications Office. We hadn't spoken since the postinaugural ball a few days earlier. While walking out of the Blue Room, the president put his hand on my shoulder and quietly whispered, "I don't want to be rude, but I gotta say . . . for a *gay* man you really are a bad dancer." Although for a moment I was embarrassed that he had noticed, I knew he was right. Wanting to make sure he knew that no offense was taken, I replied, "Mr. President, I'd be a bad dancer even if I were a *straight* man." Building on a joke can be the best way to convey to someone that you're not affronted while still keeping the moment light.

My poor dancing actually became a theme throughout my tenure. At the conclusion of the holiday photo lines, once the room was emptied of guests, I would do the "Jeremy dance." The president would join in, putting his worst foot forward. He eventually spoke of it at my going-away party on the State Floor, and when he finished his remarks, we ended up performing one last "Jeremy Dance." Pete Souza captured the moment, and it was included as one of the "Top White House Pictures" of the year.

The ability to have fun at the job was a testament to what the Obamas wanted for their staff. While they expected us to behave professionally, they also wanted us to enjoy the experience fully and to be ourselves.

LEA

George W. Bush once used his self-deprecating humor to come to the aid of my daughter. We were at a farewell dinner the Bushes threw me when I left the White House, and my daughter, Alice, then fourteen years old, was seated next to the president. He asked her how school was going, and she whispered that she was failing algebra but hadn't worked up the nerve to tell me yet. When the president heard this, he interrupted the table conversation, turned to me, and said, "Mom! Alice is flunking math, but you shouldn't worry about it because I didn't do very well in school either, and things turned out all right for me." And he raised his shoulders to indicate where we were seated, in the Yellow Oval Room with the Truman Balcony and the Washington Monument beyond. The table erupted in laughter—and no one laughed harder than Alice. Years later, when President Bush saw Alice again, he greeted her by saying, "Haven't you graduated yet?"

"I'm in college now!" she replied excitedly.

He smiled and patted her on the back. "So we both made it through."

Sometimes it can feel risky to poke fun at yourself. It makes us vulnerable, and showing vulnerability takes courage. But people recognize and admire courage in all of its forms.

FIND THE RIGHT TARGET

Humor can help foster a sense of "being in this together." Whether it's the hometown last-place baseball team or your company's biggest competitor, having a safe comic target is a useful way to build solidarity. In Washington, D.C., football fans are keenly aware of the rivalry between the Washington Redskins and the Dallas Cowboys. If you want to strike up a friendly conversation there, all you have to do is say something disparaging about the Cowboys and you'll instantly bond with most people. It's a harmless, unifying topic. The point is not to pick on a person, a group, or a country but to find an amiable way to create a connection. Just remember to be gentle; humor is more effective when it's used as a tool rather than a weapon.

LEA

For the Bushes, the holidays at the White House were a marathon of grip-and-grin receiving lines. No matter how excited they were to welcome friends and supporters to the White House, shaking hands with fourteen hundred people for five hours a day for several weeks took its toll. The Bushes smiled stoically through bear hugs and crushing handshakes as guests posed with them. For the personal aides, photographer, social aides, and me, the repetition of the photo line was mind-numbing—until the president's personal aides, Blake Gottesman and Jared Weinstein, began timing how long each greeting took. They calculated the average, and during a lull in the line, they told the Bushes that it was taking nineteen seconds per guest: they'd be standing there for another two hours. The Bushes laughed, and the president said, "Is this a new Olympic event?" It didn't change what the Bushes did, but the rest of us began racing the clock to get people through the line more quickly. We improved our times with each event. (Blake would call out the average time per guest at the end of each party to cheers or boos.)

On the night Blake announced our best time, everyone cheered, including the Bushes, because we'd shaved each photo to ten seconds, saving about twenty minutes at the end of the night. It became a running joke for us: if you asked someone if he or she had a minute, the response would be, "I can give you nineteen seconds."

Inside jokes create instant bonds. And a staff that feels bonded can accomplish much more than one that is divided and competitive.

IT'S ALL IN THE TIMING

The best humor is often based in surprise: you may think you know where a story is headed, but what makes it funny is where it actually ends up. Former Obama social secretary Julianna Smoot was chatting politely with Beyoncé and Jay-Z before a state dinner. Beyoncé was visibly nervous about her upcoming performance, and Julianna was trying to calm her. Another guest, Carlos Slim Helú, one of the wealthiest men in the world, walked past them as they stood talking. The three of them regarded Slim silently for a moment, and then Julianna said, "There goes someone even richer than you two." They all began to laugh, perhaps even harder than the joke deserved, because the unexpected humor broke the ice.

Timing can make the difference between a great laugh and an awkward moment, or worse yet, an offense. We've all taken a joke too far. Just be prepared to walk it back quickly.

JEREMY

I veered dangerously close to this situation in the fall of 2013 during the federal government shutdown. Most government workers, including many of the White House staff, were furloughed for sixteen days and could not report to work or use their work phones for any reason. On the first day after the shutdown ended, there was an event on the State Floor. As President Obama and Vice President Joe Biden waited in the Green Room, the president looked around at the various military aides, staff members, and interns and said, "It's great to have you all back! We missed you. Jeremy was running things here while you were gone, and that was a bit scary!"

Everyone laughed, including me. Wanting to continue the banter, I replied, "That's the truth. In fact, now I can work on that website issue if you need me, Mr. President." I was referring to healthcare.gov, which had been experiencing enormous problems in its early days and was drawing more attention now that the government shutdown had passed.

One of the president's assistants gasped at what I'd said, but the president laughed and put his hand on my shoulder to show he was taking it as a joke. Then everyone started laughing.

"Too soon, Mr. President?" I asked.

"Too soon." He nodded, chuckling.

I was in my fourth year at the White House at the time of this exchange and had a certain comfort level with the Obamas. But even with this joke, I added the "Too soon" as an indicator that I knew I was treading on delicate territory. If you feel you're on thin ice with a joke, you can do one of three things: be quick to reassure that you're joking out of great affection for the target, make fun of yourself for the lame joke, or change the subject. That's why we suggest you begin carefully, with safe subjects and gentle ribbing.

LEA

My husband, Wayne Berman, was working on the George H. W. Bush campaign in 1988. One day, as he was driving the campaign's chief surrogate, George W. Bush, to a meeting with supporters on Capitol Hill, he was pulled over by a policeman for having an expired license plate. Embarrassed, Wayne said, "I'm sorry, I didn't know my plate was expired, but my friend here is going to a very important meeting on the Hill, so will you let me take him there and drop him off?" Bush broke in and said, "Officer, I want to be clear: don't let him use me as an excuse. Throw the book at him!" Surprised by Bush's response, the policeman started laughing and sent them on their way.

HUMOR IS PERSUASIVE

Consider how much time you spend each day trying to convince someone to do something. Whether you're selling your spouse on the idea of buying a new car or pushing your boss to let you take over a big project at work, persuasion is a part of daily life. Making your pitch with a little humor will boost your chances of success.

JEREMY

For every enthralled guest who visited the White House, occasionally a visitor couldn't be pleased, and we would put all of our sales skills to work on that person.

When a significant supporter of the president came to a formal dinner at the White House and was shown to her table, she sought me out and said, "I don't know how you could have seated me any farther from the Obamas and still kept me in the building." I looked at her and said, "Oh, come on, you know there aren't any bad seats at the White House!" Without saying another word, I had reminded her how rare and exciting it was to be a guest of the president and first lady. She smiled and took her seat (and the hint).

Another time, I used humor to get a plan across for the typically hectic Fourth of July celebrations at the White House. In previous years, the president and Mrs. Obama had unknowingly followed the honor guard down the steps too quickly after his remarks from the balcony. This caused a bit of a jam-up once the Marine Band finished playing; as the military aide explained to me, "It didn't look clean."

For the briefing for the July Fourth event in 2012, we were all in the Blue Room together. It was a hot, sunny day, and my sunglasses were in my pocket, so I started by putting on the sunglasses with an exaggerated *Men in Black*–style gesture. Affecting a serious expression, I said, "This is a significant mission with lots of details, so I need your full attention."

The president and Mrs. Obama laughed. I explained what had happened in the past and suggested that if they could wait at the top until the honor guard got down the steps, it would be greatly appreciated. With the president and first lady at ease, a conversation that could have been awkward or patronizing became easy and effective.

I try to stay attuned to those moments when tempers are fraying and pressure is building. A well-timed quip or self-deprecating line helps raise spirits, lower blood pressure, and restore equilibrium. In the yearbooks presented to senior staff in the Obama White House at Christmas, in which the president wrote personal notes, he once wrote in mine: "To Jeremy, Thanks for the friendship, your contagious humor, and bringing fun to the White House." I was glad to hear that he felt I'd been able to balance the seriousness of the job with a lighthearted attitude.

• • •

It takes confidence to crack a joke in front of the boss (even one who isn't the president), yet that's often where a good laugh is most needed. The White House is a demanding environment, of course, but many other workplaces are highly pressured too. Think of humor and its complementary quality, charm, as wings to help you rise above the fray.

CHARM BRINGS THE WORLD TO YOU

Theodore Roosevelt was known by friends and foes alike to be irresistibly charming. Edith Wharton marveled at the impression he left on her: "He had the rare gift of bridging over in an instant those long intervals between meetings that so often benumb even the best of friends, and he was so alive at all points, and so gifted with the rare faculty of living intensely and entirely in every moment as it passed, that each moment glows in me like a tiny piece of radium." John Muir, the great naturalist, once remarked, "I fairly fell in love with him." And Woodrow Wilson admitted of his great adversary, "You can't resist the man."

Roosevelt could speak in front of almost any crowd and convince them that he was one of them. His White House was a boisterous, fun-loving place. He gave his six children and their numerous pets—including a pony, various snakes, and a badger named Josiah—full run of the house. Roosevelt also loved sports with younger staffers, playing tennis on the first White House court (which he had installed) and hosting boxing matches in the East Room. He used his charisma to create a warm and accepting environment in the White House, making it easier for him to achieve his political goals.

Like humor, charm is a crucial social skill that bridges differences of opinion and smooths the path to understanding. Have you ever noticed how one charming person can change the atmosphere of a room, or even an entire organization? It can be the newest hire or the most junior person in the office; it doesn't matter where that person is in the pecking order. They make everyone feel better. People want to help charmers; in fact, they seek out ways to aid them just because they like them.

We have identified three approaches that will have you charming everyone in your path in no time: read the room, win over with warmth, and embrace originality.

READ THE ROOM

It's easy to be charming when you're paying attention to what's going on around you. Take the temperature of a room when you enter it; if your colleagues are animated and making jokes, you know you've got a receptive audience to pitch an unusual business idea to. Bring some levity or gentle encouragement if it seems needed.

At social gatherings, be the person who makes sure no one is excluded from a dinner table conversation, or that everyone in the room has been offered a piece of cake. These small gestures make people feel cared for, and your sensitivity won't go unnoticed.

LEA

President Bush's personal aide, Blake Gottesman, was beloved by many. Blake was in his early twenties, yet he handled his heavy responsibilities and grueling schedule with style and ease, never showing fatigue or annoyance. When there were formal dinners in the State Dining Room, it was traditional to serve the deputy social secretary, Missy DeCamp, and me the same meal that the guests were having. One of the butlers would bring us beautiful plates on trays in the Usher's Office, and we would have dinner and visit with the ushers on duty. Often Blake would pop in from the Oval Office. We enjoyed his company so much, with his quick jokes and inability to say a mean thing about another person, that we started asking the butlers to bring him dinner too. We would all sit companionably in the tiny office, chatting away.

These many hours waiting outside secure meetings while leaders conduct their official duties are where real friendships grow in politics, and my friendship with Blake allowed us both to be better at our jobs because we shared information and helped each other out whenever we could. Blake knew how to couch a question so that it didn't sound like a challenge; he was always soft-spoken and swift to praise others for a job well done.

The truth is that staff members all over the White House valued Blake's opinion, went out of their way to help him, and were willing to tell him things because they trusted him. Part of his charm lay in the fact that he was full of good ideas on topics that had nothing to do with his job—for instance, his inspiration for a gift for country-western singer Kenny Chesney, who was performing at a state dinner for Prime Minister John Howard of Australia. It was customary for the president and first lady to give a personal gift to entertainers to thank them for their performance, and Blake arranged for Texas bootmaker Rocky Carroll to make Chesney a pair of fancy eel-skin boots with his initials and the flags of Australia and the United States on them. The singer was so delighted with the gift that he put the boots on the moment he got onstage that night, shaking his head in surprise and saying quietly to the audience, "The president knows what to give somebody."

Interacting with hundreds of different people each day, Blake always read the room: he took stock of people's states of mind (anxious? tongue-tied? overbearing?) and helped them in all sorts of ways to relax and feel comfortable. Simply put, he made others feel good. Though he was twenty-five years my junior, I admired and respected him. By using his powers of observation, he charmed every person he came across. As a result, he had great relationships and real influence.

WIN OVER WITH WARMTH

Warmth is a valuable element of charm. Sometimes all it takes to be warm toward someone is a small, sincere gesture. Lea once received a thank-you note from Letitia Baldrige, Jacqueline Kennedy's social secretary, which was dated "Wednesday night," after they had had lunch earlier that day. Tish had been moved to sit down and write a note of thanks just hours after the lunch, and Lea was touched by the spontaneity of her gesture.

If you hope to win others over, start with a compliment. Surely there's at least one nice thing you can think of to say when you meet someone, whether it's about that person's reputation as a hard worker or his new tie. Everyone likes to be appreciated, and it doesn't cost anything to draw attention to something positive. Giving compliments displays thoughtfulness and an open attitude, which tends to make people respond in kind. Paradoxically, the more you ask people about themselves, the better conversationalist they will think you are, because a generous person allows people to talk about themselves—and who doesn't love to do that?

Don't reserve your warmth for new acquaintances. Buy lunch for a coworker who pitched in to help you complete a big project;

clean the snow off your elderly neighbor's car in exchange for the gardening advice he gives in the summer months; or send a friend a new book by an author you know she admires. These are all thoughtful and endearing ways to show how important the people in your life are to you.

JEREMY

Carol Burnett was the recipient of the Kennedy Center Mark Twain Prize for American Humor in 2013, and the event's executive producer requested an Oval Office visit for her. The day after the ceremony, she was in the Roosevelt Room, checking her lipstick, hair, and outfit as she waited nervously for the president. The president was right on time, as usual. I opened the door leading to the small hallway where a Secret Service agent was standing at his post next to the Oval Office door. That door was closed, and then the president slowly opened it, singing, "I'm so glad we had this time together," the theme song for the comedian's long-running show. Any nervousness quickly evaporated as the president brought Carol and her family into the Oval Office. Within moments, everyone was joking and conversing with the president as if he were a longtime friend. The president was a true fan and wasn't afraid to show his sincere admiration for her. His enthusiasm—and his good voice—made everyone feel truly welcome.

Another time, I saw firsthand how warmth can turn an awkward situation into a memorable one. When I moved to California after college, I picked up catering jobs as I struggled to figure out what I was going to do "when I grew up."

I was working a party at the home of Don Rickles in Malibu. Just as the guests were arriving, I stepped onto the hot tub cover—

not considering the fact that the cover's purpose was to hold the heat in, not to keep waiters out. I immediately plunged into the warm water and jumped out almost as quickly. My coworkers saw it happen, but luckily, the guests missed it all. Nevertheless, I was horrified at being half-soaked, embarrassed that with each step my sneakers made an annoying and obvious noise. As I came to the patio to deliver drinks, Frank Sinatra, the guest of honor, yelled out, "Hey kid, what did you do, fall into the pool?"

"Yes, sir, I stepped into the hot tub," I replied as matter-of-factly as I could.

He laughed and said, "Hey, Squeaky, can you bring me an olive?" He was ribbing me, but he was also being kind. Each time I brought a drink to him, he would thank me. He asked where I was from and chatted as if we'd known each other for much longer than the two hours of the dinner. He joked with me and treated me as if I were a guest at the party, and not a waiter.

Sinatra demonstrated that being charming to someone, even if you don't know that person and may never see him again, is always worthwhile. In this case, it certainly made a lasting impression.

LEA

Warmth can be expressed in all kinds of ways. Sometimes it's about creating a sense of belonging and connection. The annual Hanukkah party at the White House was always a coveted invitation, but I'd been told that in the past, some guests hadn't eaten the food at the party because the White House kitchen was not kosher. I located a kosher caterer from Philadelphia, and he arranged for a rabbi to come to the White House on the day of the party to observe the religious traditions necessary to make the kitchen kosher. We put out discreet signs on the buffet tables to let guests know that the entire buffet was kosher. Guests were so grateful and so taken with the party that when the Marine Band struck up the traditional Jewish folk song "Hava Nagila," they joined hands and began dancing the hora in a huge circle in the Grand Foyer. When the song was over, they cheered so wildly that the band played it again and again as they danced. It was one of the greatest reactions to a party that we ever had.

EMBRACE ORIGINALITY

Once you've grown comfortable using charm in your daily life and in low-stakes situations, you can use it to come to the rescue in tense, unexpected, or emotionally charged ones. This is especially true when you make an effort to be charming in an unexpected way.

Amy Zantzinger, social secretary to President George W. Bush and Laura Bush after Lea left the White House, once witnessed a sweet and novel form of charm. One day while Amy was escorting the Dalai Lama out of the West Wing after a meeting with the president, he turned and walked up to one of the formidable-looking Marines standing at attention at the West Wing door. The Dalai Lama gently touched him under the chin and said, "Give us a little smile." The Marine looked down at the holy man in his orange robes, bearing that serene expression, and couldn't help but smile—with his eyes. Marines in the White House are like the guards at Buckingham Palace: smiling is not part of the program. The Marine's reaction was as winning as the Dalai Lama's request and created a special moment of understanding between the two of them.

JEREMY

In the days leading up to the second inauguration, the president and Mrs. Obama hosted several events at the White House that included photo receiving lines. One particular evening, Mrs. Obama was sporting a new hairstyle that had gotten a great deal of attention from the press, and I told her how much I liked it. She thanked me and said, "Ask Barack what he said about it." It turned out that the president's comment was a little less complimentary. She told me that he'd said, "It's a young cut," to which I gasped and said, "Oh my!"

The following day at another event, I was talking with the president, Mrs. Obama, and Jay Carney, the White House press secretary. The president said something to me that gave me the opportunity to jokingly reply, "Oh, you mean like the 'compliment' you gave Mrs. Obama about her haircut?" He looked at me, and in a semiserious tone to let me know it was all in fun, said, "Now, why do you bring that up? You know, you are special assistant to the president, not to the first lady. You work for me, not for her. I can fire you!"

I was standing next to Mrs. Obama and grabbed her hand and said, "Yes, but I know who has the real power in this house!" We all laughed. It was risky, but somehow I knew it would be taken the right way. At my going-away party, it was this picture, of us laughing right after my response, that they chose to present to me, with a signed inscription thanking me for being "a part of this wild ride."

A crucial part of having charm is learning to roll with it. This is especially true with the people we work or live with every day. To put it in the vernacular of baseball, you don't have to swing at every pitch; you can let a few go by now and then. You can also choose not to be too hard on yourself if something unexpected happens.

Capricia Marshall has the distinction of serving as social secretary in the Clinton White House and as chief of protocol of the United States in the Obama administration. She showed the world how to roll with it in May 2010 at a state dinner for the president of Mexico. As the motorcade arrived at the North Portico, carrying President Felipe Calderón and his wife, Margarita Zavala, with the full press corps there to capture the arrival, Capricia started down the steps to welcome them. Resplendent in a strapless pink satin gown and high heels, she slipped on the shiny marble steps, landing abruptly on her backside. There were gasps from the press as popping camera flashes nearly blinded her.

"Don't take that picture!" President Obama called out to the photographers' scrum, but the incident was captured and videos appeared online almost immediately. Capricia recovered quickly and continued down the steps, arriving just as President Calderón's car door was opened, giving the crowd a thumbs-up. She did it with panache—almost as if that was what she had been planning to do all along. Grace under pressure, as Capricia exhibited, is always winning.

THE POWER OF CHARM

If you don't know how to begin developing your own personal brand of charm, carefully watch the people you find charismatic, those who make *you* feel good whenever you encounter them. See how they behave in scenarios that make you feel tense—for instance, walking into a roomful of strangers and introducing yourself. Few social situations are more intimidating, but it's a skill that gets easier with repetition. The next step is learning how to initiate a conversation with someone you've never met. These are valuable abilities, whether you're at a summer potluck in a new neighborhood or coffee hour before an important business meeting.

Here are ways to improve your ability to connect with others in an unfamiliar setting:

Ease your way in. When you enter a crowded room, don't walk up to people who appear to be engaged in an earnest conversation. Instead, look for a loose group of people who seem to be chatting casually. Make eye contact with one of them and extend your hand. Then say, "Hello, my name is . . ." If it's a more casual setting, like a barbecue, you can go with "Hi, I'm . . ." Then shake hands with others in the group, and enter the flow of the conversation. If you caught a little of what they were discussing when you walked up, that's the best place to start: "Were you just talking about that last speaker? So powerful, didn't you think?" Or offer some tidbit of information about yourself, preferably with some humor, such as, "I'm Tom's favorite brother. Okay, his only brother."

Exit gracefully. Be comfortable disengaging from a conversation. It's not unusual to chat with a person for a short time and find you really don't have much to talk about. Just use a polite exit line such as, "It's been so nice to meet you. I hope we see each other again." Or "Will you excuse me a moment? I think I see someone I know. . . ." Or "I'm parched. Can I bring you something from the bar?" Or "Oh, there's my friend. I wondered where she went. Will you excuse me?"

Make the connection. If you forget the name of someone you just met, ask him or her to say it again. If you have to introduce a person whose name you can't remember, first introduce the person you know. Then turn to the other person and say, "Have you two met?" This gives people an opportunity to introduce themselves directly, saying their names in the process. Connect people who share similar interests. Highlight the business, friend, hometown, passion, or cause they have in common.

Don't get discouraged. If you aren't making any headway striking up a conversation with other attendees, don't take it personally. The ability to make the acquaintance of a complete stranger requires skill. If someone doesn't respond to you, he or she probably doesn't know *how* to respond. And remember that this works both ways. If someone introduces herself to you, be polite and welcoming, and engage in small talk. It's a few minutes out of your life, and it's the kind thing to do.

Go all in. When you find yourself at a dinner party seated next to someone you don't know, engage fully. You can't be charming if you're not giving that person your full attention. Make eye contact, keep your phone in your pocket or purse, and let your body language show that you're interested. Lean in, smile, and listen. It's insulting to talk to someone who is distracted or who interrupts you midsentence because she isn't really listening.

Keep it courteous. Steer away from topics that might make your dinner partner uncomfortable. If he mentions that his mother passed away recently, say you're sorry for his loss and then change the subject. If someone says something politically charged that you disagree with, you can simply say, "I don't agree" or "That's not how I see it." Again, change the subject. If the other person persists, say, "I don't think you're going to sway any minds today! Maybe we should talk about something else."

Avoid being competitive. If your dinner partner speaks glowingly of a recent trip to New York City, you could share that you were just there also, but you don't need to mention you stayed twice as long. Bragging about anything is a bad idea, especially the so-called humble brag. When we had to do seating plans for dinners at the White House, we often placed the one-uppers with one another, imagining to what heights they would go with a little competition.

Ask questions. There's almost always something useful or interesting to be learned from talking to a person, and you can make it your goal to find it. And don't finish other people's sentences for them. Some people think doing this shows that you're thinking along the same lines, but what you're really doing is taking control of the conversation rather than sharing in it.

LEA

Exercising charm can be a life-changing experience, as I learned from the way I met my husband.

The first time I saw Wayne, I was sitting in my cubicle office at the Center for Strategic and International Studies, Georgetown University's think tank, clipping articles from foreign newspapers in languages I barely knew for a researcher whose specialty was global oil reserves. It was my first job out of college; I'd just moved to Washington and didn't know a soul.

One day the door to our office suite burst open with such force that it banged against the wall. I looked up to see a plump guy headed in my direction, smiling widely under his cheesy mustache. He was wearing the largest eyeglasses I'd ever seen on a human, a short-sleeved shirt, suede Hush Puppies, and brown pants.

"Hey, I'm Wayne Berman! I just started today, working on the coal project. I saw you picking up the mail and wanted to meet you!" he said, grabbing my hand and shaking it energetically.

Oh God. I smiled slightly and responded, "Nice to meet you. I'm pretty busy here." Undaunted, he peppered me with questions: "What do you do here? Did you just graduate too? Where are you from? Do you want to get a drink after work?" It took a while to get rid of him, but that was only the beginning. He came by to chat every day.

The head of CSIS, David Abshire, seemed enthralled with Wayne and began taking him on fundraising trips to meet the center's top donors around the country. Wayne would come back and announce that he expected to receive large donations from this oilman or that newspaper publisher, and I rolled my eyes in disbelief. Then the money started coming in like it never had before. It turned out he had a keen grasp of the foreign policy substance that the donors loved and was exceptionally persuasive. The more difficult and curmudgeonly the potential donors were, the more Wayne charmed them. I came to respect his professional skills, though I still had no intention of dating him.

Over the next eighteen months, I couldn't help but notice that he was helpful, polite, funny, and kind to everyone. In fact, while I was trying to get rid of him, everyone else at CSIS was crazy about him. Eventually I was drawn in. We started dating in November and were engaged four months later.

Wayne's innate goodness and the force of his sunny personality made me fall in love with him. Of all the many blessings in my life, being married to Wayne is the greatest one of all. He taught me most of what I know about treating people well, and after thirty-five years, I still rely on him for advice about how to be charming. You never know how cultivating a little charm might pay off.

CHAPTER 3

The Quiet Strength
of Consistency

✧ ✧ ✧

There is no short cut to achievement. Life requires
thorough preparation—veneer isn't worth anything.

GEORGE WASHINGTON CARVER

B eing consistent doesn't sound very exciting. People speak
highly of mastering qualities such as confidence, honesty, and
kindness as important ways to achieve success and happiness. Yet
one of the main ingredients that determines the success or failure
of any undertaking, a key to flourishing instead of struggling, is
consistency.

Though Vice President Richard Nixon's relationship with
President Dwight Eisenhower was marred by mutual distrust and
misunderstandings, Pat Nixon was beloved by the Eisenhowers.
Mamie Eisenhower, a woman with the formidable personality of
a military wife, was in poor health during her husband's second
term. As a result, she often called on Pat Nixon to fill in for her
at White House events—sometimes with only an hour or two's
notice. Mrs. Nixon unfailingly obliged, despite having two young
daughters and her own official duties as second lady. Mrs. Eisenhower once confided to Julie Nixon Eisenhower, the Nixons'

younger daughter (who was married to the Eisenhowers' grandson, David), "Your mother was my helpmate. I never hesitated to ask her to substitute. She was always gracious and she never put on airs. She's been the Rock of Gibraltar. A good, thoroughly dependable person all her life." Stemming from a deep sense of personal obligation, Pat Nixon not only helped smooth over Nixon's prickly relationship with the president; her consistency made her an indispensable figure in the Eisenhower White House.

To become accomplished in any pursuit requires dedication. Athletes don't just decide to be good at a sport and turn into champions; they condition themselves for thousands of hours in a consistent routine. Nor does a singer take the stage without years, often decades, of practice. Remember the 10,000-hour rule, about how many hours it takes to achieve mastery in a given field, popularized by Malcolm Gladwell. Being consistent is a critical ingredient in achieving success in life because most things worth doing require time, repetition, and prolonged effort.

Consistency is more than excelling professionally. It gives strength and shape to our relationships and everything we do. Our bosses were consistent in their warmth and graciousness, which informed all of their interactions and had a powerful effect on everyone they encountered. Mrs. Obama was always exquisitely turned out, yet she made a point of being approachable. Kids especially felt comfortable hugging her immediately. President Obama has a contagious smile and laugh that made guests feel at home. Laura Bush put people at ease by asking them about their lives, always scanning the fringes of a party to see if anyone seemed left out and sending staff to bring them over for a chat. President Bush is gregarious and comfortable around people; he has a knack for bestowing fun nicknames and teasing his friends. When he was particularly impressed with a person, he would call after them, "You're a good man" or "You're a good woman." That kind of consistent civility builds bridges and makes people feel cared for.

Consistency is also a crucial ingredient for a happy family life. If you tell your son or daughter that you will come to their basketball game or concert, your presence at these events, however challenging that can sometimes be, shows that you're dependable and you prioritize them. Being consistent is a form of thoughtfulness, especially with the people you care about the most.

Personal reputations are built on consistency. When your behavior reflects your words and promises, people know what to expect and they appreciate and remember you for it. Inconsistency and a failure to follow through are common human faults. Sometimes we don't like what we're supposed to be doing, we don't feel well, or we're just not in the mood. But when we don't show up or otherwise fulfill our commitments, we let others down and that can alter how they see us. There is no trust without consistency.

How we are perceived is important. If customers like a store but the hours of operation are erratic and they arrive to find it closed a few times, they'll go somewhere else. An employee who repeatedly misses deadlines is not going to be given more responsibility or the chance to move up. Many people now, succumbing to the infinite distractions of modern life, seem incapable of committing to much of anything. Their Fear of Missing Out causes them to miss the moment. We were amazed that even an invitation to the White House is often treated casually. It's worth thinking about one's priorities. If the prospect of agreeing to a simple lunch with a good friend feels like a stifling commitment, it might be time to ask yourself why. After all, if you develop a reputation for being around only when *you* need something, people will grow to think of you as a fair-weather friend and will value your opinions and your company less.

Consistency requires you to do things even if you don't feel like it. It takes willpower. It also takes practice, the formation of a habit that you'll eventually no longer need to think about. We have found that the four most important elements of consistency are to create efficient routines, be decisive, anticipate the unexpected, and become a closer.

MAKE IT ROUTINE

A state dinner was scheduled for the week after President Nixon's resignation in August 1974. President Gerald Ford, eager to return the White House to normalcy as quickly as possible, determined that the dinner should still take place and added some of his own guests to the list. Despite the enormous upheaval in the White House, Nixon's social secretary, Lucy Breathitt, stayed to help the Fords through their first big social obligation, putting aside her personal sadness for the Nixons to bring the event off brilliantly. Social secretaries often form close personal bonds with the first ladies they serve, and Lucy must have gone about her duties in those last days in the White House with a heavy heart. But she got on with her responsibilities and made the dinner a success. The execution of White House state dinners was a well-established routine, and it was important to signal that nothing, not even the unexpected departure of a president, could interrupt the tradition.

People are more comfortable when they know what to expect. Routines are key in providing a workplace structure in which employees and supervisors can work together in mutual trust. We're not just talking about practices that improve work flow or ensure productivity. It is equally important to establish good habits for your day-to-day interactions with people. If colleagues see you treating every person with the same attention and respect, they'll be more likely to communicate potential problems or opportunities, and when you regularly consult them in the development of company goals, you establish a confidence-building sense of cooperation.

Having a routine allows us to focus on other parts of the day that require our full attention, knowing that the basics have been covered. If children know that when they come home from school, there will be a snack, then homework, play, dinner, a little television perhaps, a bath, a story, and bedtime, you're giving them a structure they can rely on. You're setting them up to thrive. But consistency isn't just for child care. We are all hardwired to find structure comforting.

LEA

From the day that I began at the White House, the residence staffers were kind and welcoming as individuals, but they were part of an entrenched bureaucracy that had its own way of doing things. I'd ask for the carpet on the East Room stage to be cleaned, for example, or for fading flowers to be removed from the State Floor floral arrangements before they started dropping petals—little things that guests should expect of a White House event. But I began to see that some of my requests and new ideas were given lip service and then politely ignored; it was easier for a staffer to say something had "slipped through the cracks" than to actually carry out changes.

I decided to start making daily rounds to the back rooms and service areas of the White House, following Mrs. Bush's lead in being sure to keep every interaction friendly and encouraging. I visited the staffer who had been asked to implement a new way of doing something and asked politely about progress every day until he or she realized I wasn't going to stop. Once people knew what the routine was—that he or she would be seeing me daily and I'd be requesting a progress update—things did begin to change. It may have been annoying to some and it wasn't my favorite task either, but it got the attention of the staff. Eventually it became easier for people to do what I asked rather than to keep making excuses. Establishing that custom helped me accomplish my goals.

JEREMY

I also found myself implementing new procedures. The Social Office had been holding staff meetings, but not necessarily on a daily basis and the times always varied, depending on the day's events. I realized it was important to have a morning meeting at a set time, even if some staff were engaged in an event. A regularly scheduled gathering meant that I could relay any announcements from the senior staff meeting earlier that morning, as well as do a postmortem on the previous day's events to discuss what went right as well as any lessons learned. It was a good way for our team to be on the same page before starting the day.

Here are some tips for establishing productive routines:

Set up systems. These help everyone on staff communicate better. Holding standardized meetings each week where everyone is asked to talk about what they're working on creates an expectation of progress between one meeting and the next.

Even a group coffee break can be a useful way to stay connected informally.

Reset the clock. Show up on time in the morning. If you're a manager, be clear about standard working hours. Also state exactly how early you expect staff to show up for a meeting or an event.

Check in. Ask about any particularly challenging projects coworkers are involved in. Inquire how a meeting went. In this way you show you're interested in what your colleagues are doing and you want to be helpful.

BE DECISIVE

The Obamas decided from the start of the administration that they would have a different take on the social arena and not participate in the DC social scene as many of their predecessors had done. Instead, they put a clear emphasis on kids—both their own and others.

On most nights, the president sat down to dinner with his family at 6:30 p.m., a deliberate effort to create a sense of normalcy and stability for his daughters. As Valerie Jarrett, a senior advisor to President Obama, told the History Channel, "By six-fifteen, I'm looking up at the clock and going, 'We better wrap it up here,' because [Michelle] will not hold dinner. She doesn't want to make the children sit there and wait for him. And he respects that. And I think something as simple as that, to create this sense that the children are the most important thing in their life, even though he has the most powerful job in the world, is really important."

The Obamas also put a lot of effort into having schoolchildren from the region visit the White House. Holidays like Halloween became an official staple event, with local students coming to the

White House for trick-or-treating. It was a conscious and unmistakable decision that their focus was going to be different from that of other administrations.

Decisiveness is a critical leadership skill, but it can be challenging to put into practice. We rarely had a moment to mull over our decisions, and that's not unique to the White House; most of us hurtle through life without time for thoughtful consideration about our choices.

When faced with a decision, it's important to examine the possibilities thoroughly, consider the potential negative effects (and how you will deal with them), but don't dither once you know what needs to be done. The failure to make a decision *is* a decision. When people—especially bosses—waver about what to do, they inject stress into the situation and cause people to question their judgment because they are clearly not sure of it themselves. Indecisiveness can cause existing problems to fester and grow, creating a whole new set of issues to resolve. Social secretaries know how to make things happen quickly: there aren't many procrastinators among us because wasting time was a luxury we never had.

Here are some suggestions for how to act decisively:

Give a deadline for providing input. When you need to make a decision at work, listen politely to your colleagues' ideas and concerns, but don't commit to anything before you've weighed all your options. Once you've chosen a path, make it clear that the decision cannot be revisited.

Share your conclusion. In this way, everyone has the same information you do. State what you're doing in the positive, even if the decision you're making is the result of a setback or failure. If you have a change of heart over a pending deal with a client, let her know as soon as possible. It's unprofessional to leave her hanging and holds up her choices about what to do next.

Stick to it. Being capricious is costly, both financially and in terms of personal reputation. That doesn't mean you shouldn't make changes when you see that something isn't working, but have the courage to give your choices a chance. We've both hired staff for whom we had high hopes, only to be disappointed at first. We didn't give up on them; we pointed out what was lacking and reminded them of our expectations. Usually the extra attention and patience paid off, and we were rewarded with valued team members.

Start with small decisions at home. For example, what color to paint your bedroom. Give yourself a time limit—say, fifteen minutes—to make your choice. Then move on to larger decisions, like where to go on summer vacation or what to get your significant other for his or her birthday, breaking these decisions up into parts at first if you get stuck. You're building the skills to make larger and more significant life decisions more comfortably and confidently.

ANTICIPATE THE UNEXPECTED

We can't predict all the ways that something can go wrong, but, like creating routines and being decisive, considering possible scenarios will make you more ready and responsive. You can be consistent even if life isn't. We had to be ready for the unexpected with every White House event. In April 2006, when a heckler interrupted the arrival ceremony of the president of China, Lea saw firsthand what can happen when there isn't a plan in place.

That morning, as I was standing in the Diplomatic Reception Room trying to get a glimpse of the event on the South Lawn, I was already feeling as if my head was about to explode because I'd just heard the White House announcer introduce the president of the People's Republic of China as "the president of the Republic of China." This was an insult to the Chinese; the Republic of China is *Taiwan*. And while it was an honest mistake, it was deeply embarrassing.

Suddenly a State Department protocol officer ran down the hall and shouted hysterically at me, "There's a heckler! The Chinese think we did it on purpose!" As she sped past me, I raced to the doors to find out what was happening and could see a commotion at the far end of the South Lawn as the Secret Service was hustling a man off the grounds. The heckler had been admitted on a press pass and at first appeared to be one of five thousand happy visitors waving American and Chinese flags on the South Lawn. Neither the Secret Service nor the Communications Office had a contingency plan for hecklers, and it took several long minutes before he was finally removed, with President Hu Jintao and his delegation growing increasingly angry and embarrassed. Strike two with the Chinese.

When the arrival ceremony ended, everything began to happen at once: the protocol officer reappeared to tell me that key members of the Chinese delegation were dropping out of the luncheon in protest, and just when I thought things couldn't get any worse, the Chinese president's interpreter shoved President Bush's interpreter out of her seat behind the head table. I'd been warned by the State Department that this might happen and was told to prevent it; it was essential that President Bush have his own translator for his private conversation. The two presidents were already arriving at the East Room as I argued politely but fruitlessly with the Chinese interpreter. I pulled the American interpreter close to the seat and said, "When I get this seat open, you sit in it, and don't get up for anything until this lunch is over." Then I tipped the Chinese interpreter's chair forward a few inches, and she leaped up and whirled on me in anger. I quickly slid the chair away from her and pushed the American interpreter into it. The Chinese chief of protocol rushed at me in fury at my very inappropriate behavior, but I was literally saved by the Marine Band, which struck up "Hail to the Chief" at that moment. The two presidents arrived at their seats—and the incident was over. The Chinese interpreter had no alternative but to sit in the chair provided for her, behind her president.

It was my worst day as a social secretary, unlike anything I'd ever experienced before. When I saw the film of the arrival ceremony and the stony look on President Bush's face, I was ashamed: we had let him down. I knew the incident couldn't have helped smooth the negotiations taking place that day. After that, we put plans in place to avoid a repeat of the situation.

When it comes to establishing yourself as a consistent problem solver, visualizing the possibilities and having a backup plan are key. This may sound like daydreaming, but sitting quietly and thinking over all the aspects of a situation and imagining how it might go is a great way to prevent trouble. If you're giving a presentation before a meeting and are using equipment, test it in advance (it's amazing how many people skip this step). If you're speaking in front of a group, time your remarks so you know if they should be longer or shorter. Rehearse your speech ahead of the meeting so your message is clear and concise. And if you're dealing with a potentially contentious issue, schedule a premeeting with trusted colleagues to go over any potential rough spots.

It's never possible to anticipate all unexpected situations, of course, but our responses in such moments still need to be consistent and reasonable. Weather calls for White House events were a nightmare; from state dinners in the Rose Garden to the Congressional Picnic with a thousand people on the South Lawn, we were the ones choosing to cancel an event because of threatening weather or to brazen it out and hope for the best. Whatever happened, though, our bosses knew we'd be ready with answers and options.

JEREMY

For a state dinner set for early summer, the calligraphers found amazing photos of a 1982 state dinner for the president of the Philippines that the Reagans hosted in the Rose Garden. After discussing the idea with Mrs. Obama, we decided to have the dinner in the Rose Garden as well. Preparations for a gorgeous summer evening event had been coming together for months. In the days leading up to it, Max Doebler, who was tracking the weather in the Military Office, informed us that a shower was approaching. All indications were that it would dissipate miles away from Washington, but it left us with a 20 percent chance of rain. A decision had to be made by 7:00 a.m. on the day of the event. There was no time or budget for a tent, even if we wanted one. That morning, on a conference call with the Protocol Office at the State Department, the Secret Service, the Military Office, and numerous others, I kept thinking of the phrase "When in doubt, don't," but something made me take a chance.

Once I made my decision, we all moved forward with the planning. I probably spent as much time gazing at the sky for rainclouds that evening as I did looking people in the eye and greeting them. Thankfully, the rain arrived around 3:00 a.m., hours after the guests departed.

LEA

When I postponed the Congressional Picnic for one day because of imminent thunderstorms, some members of Congress deluged the White House with angry complaints: "My kids were missing school for this!" "I invited my dentist and my neighbor, and they can't come tomorrow!" Then the worst thing happened: the threatening clouds moved off and the promised storm never materialized. My afternoon was spent making apology calls for the good weather. I couldn't control the weather, but I could acknowledge that the complaints had been heard and that we sincerely regretted the difficulties caused by the decision. As we'll learn in chapter 9, when you make the wrong call, it's best to accept responsibility, do what it takes to fix things, and then move on.

Whenever we had a state arrival ceremony at the White House, we had a contingency plan for moving it inside for inclement weather. We all lived in dread of what would be a big disappointment to the thousands of people coming to the South Lawn to see the arrival, but the military honor guard and key members of the arrival ceremony always practiced a Grand Foyer arrival-and-welcome indoors just in case. Deesha Dyer took over the position of social secretary from Jeremy in May 2015, and one of her first projects was organizing a Girl Scout campout on the South Lawn. It was an idea inspired by Mrs. Obama's Let's Move! initiative.

Since the White House is considered a national park, the grounds are operated by the National Park Service, which falls under the jurisdiction of the Department of the Interior. The secretary of the interior, Sally Jewell, was very excited about the camping idea. As usual, planning this occasion required the full cooperation of many parts of the White House—among them, the First Lady's Office, the Secret Service, the White House Military Office, the White House Medical Unit, and the executive residence staff.

Deesha was determined to make this event a reality. The plan was that fifty girls would be welcomed to the White House, play games, have scavenger hunts, pitch tents, eat dinner, and sing campfire songs with the president and Mrs. Obama before heading to bed in their tents on the South Lawn. A real campfire with open flames on the lawn was not possible, so battery-operated lanterns were proposed instead. After checking and triple-checking that everything would be safe and fun for the girls, Mrs. Obama signed off on the idea.

The day arrived, and all was going as planned—until the issue cropped up that haunts all social secretaries no matter the era: the weather gods stepped in. Deesha had been in close contact with the Military Office, which was monitoring the weather and reporting threats of rain. Knowing this was always a possibility, she had the girls rehearse what to do in case of a storm: if they heard a loud whistle, they were to throw their belongings in their bags and proceed to the Diplomatic Room of the White House. There, chaperones and Secret Service agents would guide them to the Eisenhower Office Building, where a makeshift sleeping room had been prepared.

Just as it looked as if all was well, there were reports of lightning miles away, but still too close for comfort. All divisions of the White House agreed to evacuate the South Lawn and move everyone inside. The diligent Girl Scouts followed directions perfectly. None of them seemed to mind; in fact, the drama may have made the evening even more exciting. The next morning, the kids woke up early and had breakfast, as planned, before heading out of the White House. That night was nerve-racking for Deesha, but she still considers it one of her favorite memories.

JEREMY

Having a good backup plan means quick thinking and a little luck. Some people have a recurring nightmare about showing up for an exam that they forgot to study for or finding themselves at the wheel of a runaway car. My nightmare was that the entertainment for a White House event would cancel at the last minute. And one day, it happened.

It was always a thrill to make the initial call approaching talent for an event. If it was someone we had not dealt with previously, the manager or agent would often ask incredulously: "Is this really the White House?" Then we confirmed that the talent was interested and available, and we discussed our budget constraints. It wasn't unusual to have some negotiating at this stage, but almost everyone felt it was an honor to perform at the White House, despite the fact that limited funds were available. There is no binding contract with the White House because there is no payment for entertainers and only minimal funds to cover costs such as travel, hotel, and equipment.

Gahl Hodges Burt, one of President Reagan's social secretaries, warned me over lunch that at some point an entertainer would cancel with little notice; it happens in every administration. Much to my dismay, Gahl's prediction came true for one of Mrs. Obama's favorite events, the Kids' State Dinner, pioneered by Sam Kass, the executive director of her Let's Move! initiative. For the 2012 event, the White House teamed up with the Department of Education and the Department of Agriculture to ask kids ages eight to twelve to submit original recipes as part of the Healthy Lunchtime Challenge. Fifty-four young "chefs" from each state (and territories and the District of Columbia) were selected and invited to bring a parent or guardian and attend the lunch with Mrs. Obama. The decor and entertainment were very much a priority for Mrs. Obama; this was as important for her as any actual state dinner.

In 2014, the entertainer of choice was an immensely popular singer and producer whose upbeat hit song was being played incessantly across the country. We called his team to see if he would come, and he accepted. We had numerous conversations regarding the budget, and no problems were evident. But a week before the event, the contact person suddenly informed me that there were additional requests. We immediately started thinking about a backup, though at that point, we believed things would be resolved.

Luck can be an important element in worst-case scenarios, and we were indeed lucky. *The Lion King* was currently playing at the Kennedy Center. We connected with Disney to invite the cast to perform, and by that evening we had a viable plan B. There were no timing conflicts and the Kennedy Center was just a few blocks away, so travel wasn't an issue, but I hadn't discussed the situation with Mrs. Obama. I didn't want to present her with the prospect of a new plan unless we were sure we would be losing the star. I made several calls to the performer's team, but it wasn't until Sunday morning that we actually spoke; the event was on a Friday. I was shocked by the asks: a private jet to and from Los Angeles instead of the first-class ticket originally agreed on, a cast of more than sixty dancers, and additional demands that made the entire idea implausible. Even if the costs weren't an issue, there wasn't room for that many people unless we disinvited the guests! I pressed for more information. I was informed that the performance would not take place unless we agreed to everything. I explained that it would be impossible to ever fulfill such requests at the White House. We couldn't come to terms. I never knew if the celebrity was aware of the situation.

Now I had to put the backup plan in place. I had already given a heads-up of the possible conflict to Tina Tchen, Mrs. Obama's chief of staff. I emailed Mrs. Obama and explained the situation as concisely as possible. She was far from happy and asked many of the same questions I had posed when the additional demands were made. How could someone make a commitment, especially for an event with kids at the White House, and suddenly cancel? Had we not been clear about details or budget? I tried to be honest without saying, "It's their fault, not mine." (When something goes wrong, it's never a good idea to try to pass the buck.) After some back-and-forth, Mrs. Obama wrote that I should "check with Barack in the morning. He has some ideas." Yikes.

Exactly what world issues were occurring at the time I don't remember, but I do recall dreading that conversation. It wouldn't work to do my usual morning stop-by in the outer Oval Office and hope the president would come out to chat. I called his assistant, and she promised to get back to me. Within minutes she called back—with the president on the line. When he heard about all the additional requests, he agreed that our backup plan was the way to go and asked me to tell Mrs. Obama. I wasn't looking forward to conveying that message. Mrs. Obama was traveling, so I had to email the update. A staff member traveling with the first lady questioned how I had screwed this up and asked how long I'd had the information and not shared it. I couldn't focus on defending myself; I had to convince the first lady that my backup plan would work. I don't know if I was successful in that effort, but a few days later, the cast of *The Lion King* convinced her themselves by putting on an amazing show, which the kids loved. Afterward, I walked with Mrs. Obama down the red-carpeted hallway as we exited the East Room. Balloons in the shapes of various animals festooned the hall instead of the flowers that would normally be in place for a state dinner. Mrs. Obama turned to me and said, "That was perfect. *That* was a better choice."

It can be challenging and frustrating, but being prepared for an unexpected situation is better than being caught off guard without a clue as to what to do next.

BECOME A CLOSER

In your quest for consistency, you've established routines, practiced being decisive, and learned to be ready for anything. Now it's time to seal the deal by being a closer: a person who stays with a project until it's truly done.

Consistency builds over time, but you can lose it quickly if you can't live up to your promises. In being consistent, as in so many other areas, accountability is a powerful motivator. If we assured our first ladies that invitations would be out by a certain date or that guests would be assembled in the East Room by a specific time, you can believe we made those things happen.

Learning to finish what you start is hard—but even more difficult than finishing something is to keep starting over and over. Nothing much happens when you begin a project; progress comes with sustained effort. Be kind to yourself, proceed gradually, and do the small things you can manage every day rather than making an extreme effort that isn't tenable. If you need to, ask for help—don't be shy about enlisting the aid of others to help keep you on track.

LEA

When I worked for Lynne Cheney as the social secretary and house manager of the vice president's residence, there was so much renovation work to be done to the big white Victorian house on the Naval Observatory grounds that the Cheneys were not able to move in until six weeks after the inauguration. While the house was under renovation, I worked with Mrs. Cheney and her interior designer to furnish it. In addition to the Cheneys' own furniture, we had a small array of sad-looking pieces that came with the residence, but it wasn't nearly enough to furnish the public spaces of the house.

I knew that the State Department had an inventory of fine American antiques, and I appealed to them to let us borrow several items, and a nonprofit residence foundation raised funds to buy things like lamps, sofas, and carpeting. Mrs. Cheney strategically placed her antiques around the house, but the walls were bare. I called the National Gallery of Art, and we went to look at paintings the gallery had in storage that we might borrow, a common practice offered to various White House offices. The pickings were slim; in fact, everything we requested seemed to be unavailable for one reason or another.

The next stop was the Smithsonian's National Museum of American History, which parted with three fabulous George Catlin paintings. We were making headway, but there was still a lot of empty wall space. I cast the net wider, and we visited the Corcoran Gallery of Art and the Phillips Collection; each loaned a painting.

Our biggest challenge was an enormous, bare living room wall. One day Mrs. Cheney came to my office at the back of the house with a book about the artist Helen Frankenthaler. She showed me a photo of a cool green painting, *Lush Spring*, and said, "This is exactly the kind of thing we need for the living room." I saw in the caption that the painting was hanging in the Phoenix Art Museum. Getting that painting was a long shot, but it was worth a few calls to investigate. Just because something hasn't been done before doesn't mean it can't be done.

I called the head of the museum, James Ballinger, introduced myself, and asked if he would loan the painting to the vice president's residence. He was very surprised to be asked for a multiyear loan of such a valuable painting but promised to inquire and get back to me soon, and he did: the Frankenthaler painting, he said, was coming to the residence. When I told Mrs. Cheney, she was surprised and delighted. *Lush Spring* was installed in a place of honor for the duration of the Cheneys' time in the residence, and they even hosted a dinner in honor of Helen Frankenthaler to celebrate the loan, raising awareness of this brilliant American artist. I kept reaching out to museums all over the United States, and we were able to borrow and showcase some exceptional American art in the vice president's residence. It took nine months to fully furnish the house, but it was well worth the effort to keep searching for art, one great painting at a time. The house was featured in *Architectural Digest* in 2001, with an article about the renovation written by Lynne Cheney herself.

Here are some thoughts about how to be a good closer:

Begin simply. Start by forcing yourself to do the things that bother you the least; it's almost never as bad as you think it will be, and you'll gain momentum. Work up to the ones you dislike the most, and congratulate yourself for doing the right thing. You're seeing something through and building a reliable reputation.

Be specific. If you're clear about what you want to achieve, you're far more likely to succeed. This is especially true in the business world. Would you like to reach a sales goal that has eluded you until now? Focus on exactly what needs to be done: answer every call from every client in a timely fashion; ask your regular clients for referrals; give your repeat customers a small discount in return for their valued patronage. Looking for specific solutions and then applying yourself to them consistently may be the difference between the status quo and finally breaking through to another level of performance.

Don't get distracted. When you feel worn down by backbiting or disengaged colleagues at work, remind yourself of what you want to accomplish and power through those unhelpful encounters to meet the specific goal you've set for yourself. Maintaining focus will push you over the finish line with or without them.

Finish what you start. Whether it's working on a project with a fast-approaching deadline or spending an afternoon with your least favorite family member, we all have obligations we'd like to skip. Resist the impulse. If you've accepted an invitation to a party, don't assume that no one will notice if you don't show up. If everyone thought that way, every party would be guest-free.

Variety may be the spice of life, but save it for trying out a new restaurant or including a new color in your wardrobe. No one wants a wildly unpredictable colleague or sporadically invested best friend.

CONSISTENCY COUNTS

It's amazing what can be accomplished with unremitting dedication. George W. Bush's constant, decades-long fight against AIDS is considered one of his greatest legacies. In 2003, George W. Bush announced the President's Emergency Plan For AIDS Relief (PEPFAR), a $15 billion, five-year program to introduce treatment to fight AIDS in Africa. PEPFAR is the largest international health initiative to fight a single disease ever created, and it has delivered treatment to more than 11.5 million people. His commitment to fighting disease in Africa didn't stop when he left office; it expanded to draw attention to the need for the treatment of breast and cervical cancer. The Bushes have made many trips to Africa since leaving the White House, continuing to work toward a goal of eradicating AIDS by 2030, and their ongoing humanitarian efforts have saved many lives. The power of consistency can change the world.

CHAPTER 4

Listen First, Talk Later

✦ ✦ ✦

*I'm a very strong believer in listening
and learning from others.*

RUTH BADER GINSBURG

L istening with your full attention can be hard, especially when we have so many distractions. Can you remember the last time someone turned away from his or her devices and gave you their complete focus? When you listen quietly to another person, you're sending a powerful message: that his or her words are more important to you than anything else. It's a sign of respect and regard. The presidents and first ladies we worked for understood that.

Active listening, which both the State Department and the FBI recommend, is the process of listening with focus, a lack of prejudgment, and your undivided attention. It helps you build trust and rapport with your colleagues while improving your own chances of being heard. Good listeners put the speaker's needs ahead of their own. Listening is an exercise in patience and humility, and like the other skills you've begun to master, it's a talent that anyone who puts in the effort can acquire.

We live in a world of constant communication but lackluster listening. The more we multitask, the less we hear, and yet the more quickly we expect others to respond. Suddenly, genuine listening seems nearly impossible, but it's not, and here's why you should try it.

Charisma isn't just about charm and personality: gifted listeners possess a quiet force that draws people toward them, inviting intimacy, loyalty, and truthfulness. So what do great listeners have in common? They're self-aware but empathetic: they can see the world through the eyes of others, which gives them a better understanding of what the speaker is saying. And taking things in thoughtfully allows good listeners to find the right words in a conversation, to be helpful rather than heedless.

Ray LaHood, a Republican congressman from Illinois, became the US secretary of transportation in 2009. In a time of extreme partisanship, it wasn't the fact that he was a Republican serving in the cabinet of a Democrat that made him stand out but how he changed the morale of the agency. When he started, the Department of Transportation was ranked last among the large agencies for employee satisfaction and commitment. LaHood wanted to find out firsthand the causes for the dissatisfaction. He went to highway and transit offices as well as to air traffic control towers around the country. The employees were surprised; few had ever had a secretary visit them before. During these visits, he listened to their concerns. His first step was to gather information and get a grasp of the most pressing issues.

He also focused on follow-through. Under his leadership, the agency implemented a town hall meeting that was live-streamed so workers from across the country could participate. It provided a means for them to share issues and ideas and for leadership to listen. By the time LaHood departed as secretary in 2013, the agency was rated the most improved for employee satisfaction, according to the *Washington Post*'s "Best Places to Work in Federal Government."

There's a powerful advantage to being a good listener: it's a telegraphed form of respect that helps build friendships and solid working relationships. One really good conversation can completely transform the behavior and inspire the cooperation of others. In previous chapters, we've shown how relationships are often built on a base of confidence and consistency, and that adding a little charm and good humor helps you make meaningful connections. Careful listening is another element in your plan to treat people better every day. We've come up with six ways you can improve your listening skills: listen with care, develop empathy, embrace silence, look between the lines, funnel sensitive matters, and stay open-minded.

LISTEN WITH CARE

Paying attention establishes that you care about what a person is saying and, by extension, that you care about that person. It takes concentration and restraint to listen carefully, focus on the important ideas being expressed, and refrain from forming your reply until the speaker is finished. And when you don't like the message—*especially* when you don't like the message—it's critical not to shoot the messenger. If we had jumped down the throats of our staff every time they had bad news—like telling us they were being deluged with calls from people RSVPing to a dinner to which they hadn't been invited—we would never have been able to fix the actual problem. Also, if we'd attacked them every time they brought us a problem, our staff would have been afraid to tell us what was really going on.

Besides the altruistic benefits, listening can become a survival mechanism, especially in a competitive workplace. When we worked at the White House, we quickly figured out that the more we asked questions about every event we planned, the better prepared we would be to make it exceptional. We listened carefully so that we could understand exactly what the presidents and first ladies wanted for their guests. Even when the constraints of their schedules made it impossible for them to communicate every detail, we noted and followed the patterns of how they liked things to be done, and our jobs became easier over time as we learned their preferences. Lea knew that the Bushes would be early for every event, so she made sure that everything was in place fifteen minutes before start time. Jeremy knew to confirm that either he or someone from his staff was always within view of the president or Mrs. Obama in case they needed something. If he had to walk away or be absent from an event, he would remind his staff to stand close by.

We often acted as intermediaries, communicating our bosses' wishes to other staff members. When you're in that role, some staffers won't always comprehend that the requests are coming from the principals and have nothing to do with your own personal desires. In our case, it made for some challenges to our authority in the beginning, but eventually our colleagues recognized that if the president and first lady trusted us, they could too.

LEA

In May 2005, Mrs. Bush hosted a luncheon for fashion designer Oscar de la Renta, which was scheduled to coincide with a visit from Nancy Reagan. I was particularly nervous about this high-profile event because Mrs. Reagan's guest list included people like Anna Wintour of *Vogue*, Annette de la Renta, and Barbara Walters. I wanted the luncheon to be perfect and pored through cookbooks to find just the right entrée, an elegant little pastry basket that looked like a lobster pot, constructed over individual servings of lobster stew. I consulted with the new executive chef, Cristeta Comerford, and she was enthusiastic.

On the day of the luncheon, when the lobster was served, it looked nothing like the photo I'd shown Cris. It tasted great, but it looked like lobster stew. I was crushed; I didn't want anyone thinking Laura Bush had chosen and approved this fairly ordinary-looking dish. I knew that having lunch in the family quarters at the White House with a current and a former first lady was a truly special occasion, but it's easy in a high-pressure job to get obsessed with the one little thing that went wrong rather than appreciate the many other things that were right.

Crestfallen, I went to Cris afterward and asked in as measured a tone as I could muster, "What happened to the pastry basket that was supposed to be on top of the lobster? That was so special and pretty." Cris seemed confused: "I thought you just wanted us to use the recipe—not the presentation." It was an honest miscommunication, and my disappointment doubled when I saw that Cris felt she'd let *me* down. After that, we got a lot more specific and really listened attentively to one another. Of course, Laura Bush never mentioned it to either of us, but I'd bet she noticed, and just went along with it. (First ladies and other charming and highly effective figures know when to speak up and when to look the other way when a mistake can't be undone.)

DEVELOP EMPATHY

To be a good listener, you have to be interested in the world around you. Former president Bill Clinton wrote in his memoir, "I learned that everyone has a story—of dreams and nightmares, hope and heartache, love and loss, courage and fear, sacrifice and selfishness. All my life I've been interested in other people's stories. I wanted to know them, understand them, feel them." That deep-seated wish to connect with others is part of what made Clinton such an intuitive and successful politician: people felt that he really engaged with the issues affecting their lives.

Sympathy sets us above another person's problem, whereas empathy puts us on the same level. If you're empathetic while you listen, you're not judging; you're simply trying to understand what someone else feels. Each of us has experienced a time when we felt ignored or not valued. The difference we feel when we're acknowledged and included is immense. That stark contrast is what makes empathy so important.

JEREMY

Mrs. Obama made sure every initiative she embraced was carefully considered before taking it on as one of her priorities. In 2011, Mrs. Obama, along with Dr. Jill Biden, launched Joining Forces, which supported service members, veterans, and their families by providing resources for employment, education, and wellness.

The first lady was extremely aware of the challenges that face service members and veterans and also the problems their families encounter. She admitted that her perspective on the initiative differed significantly from that of Dr. Biden, who had a son serving in the military. Mrs. Obama did not have that connection, but she learned from spending time with military families. She heard about how each move to another base created job relocation issues, as well as difficulties for children moving from one school to another. As she traveled the country and her understanding grew, so did the initiative, which eventually included a mental health public awareness campaign. Because she discussed what she discovered with staff at regular meetings, the empathy she developed for those she encountered provided a road map for her goals.

WHY SILENCE REALLY IS GOLDEN

To listen well, first clear away all distractions: reading materials, phones, tablets. You're letting the speaker know that she has your undivided attention. Second, research has shown that we think much faster than we speak. This means that while you're trying hard to listen to something important that person is telling you, you're probably thinking about several other things at the same time—what to say in response, how to carry out what the person you're speaking with is suggesting, what to have for lunch—when what you really should be doing is *just listening* to what's actually being said. It takes self-discipline, but don't formulate your reply until the speaker has finished talking.

Silence is powerful; taking a moment to think over your response shows that you are sincerely considering what's been said. Don't let a quiet pause make you uncomfortable; give yourself some time to understand what's being put forth.

There is an established correlation between listening and leadership; the best leaders listen more than they speak and often allow others to come to conclusions on their own simply by asking the right questions. President John F. Kennedy's daily appointments seldom lasted longer than fifteen minutes. People who met with him recount that he generally said little for the first ten minutes or so, listening intently to what his visitor had to say without "sounding off." He would save his volley of questions for the last five minutes, before politely but firmly escorting his visitor out the door.

Listening is also a useful sales technique. The best salespeople ask their customers what they want and attend closely to the response. We always asked guests what they especially liked on the White House buffets so that we could continue to serve the top crowd pleasers. (The enduring favorites were shrimp cocktail, baked ham, and the eggnog at Christmas, which was more potent than a double martini.)

Letting people talk requires us to listen empathetically, but it also demands that we maintain a healthy handle on our own emotions. When we hear things that challenge our personal beliefs and convictions, we tend to stop listening and start rebutting in our heads. But too much emotion, however well intended, inhibits logical thinking. Staying in the moment and really *hearing* the other person allows the possibility of true understanding.

When it's finally your turn to talk, ask specific questions to show you've been paying close attention and request clarification of anything that you didn't understand. Reference some of the other person's comments and use her own words as you begin to formulate your response.

When someone uses vague expressions like "Nobody ever tells me what's going on around here," ask for specific examples: What exactly do you need to know that's not being communicated? How many times has this happened? One can be a more effective problem solver by knowing the layout of a situation.

It's helpful to list the areas in which you're in agreement because it builds consensus. When the other person realizes that you're on the same page, you can then point out areas where your views diverge. Be clear as you explain why. Then get ready to begin the process again. You'll find your conversations become easier and more productive.

Just as you strive to take things in calmly, be patient with those who are listening to you. If you're sharing difficult or sensitive information, allow them time to absorb what you're saying. Don't expect an immediate reaction. Sometimes people need space and a little peace and quiet before they're ready to respond.

JEREMY

Years ago I became keenly aware of how important it is to let others absorb information when sharing something sensitive or important, and to provide the time to allow them to digest it. It was when I was coming out and telling my family and friends that I was gay. Throughout my youth, I had tried to ignore my sexuality. I was terrified that the truth would be discovered, and at that point I didn't know how my family would react.

As years passed and I entered adulthood, I slowly came out, but it was very compartmentalized. I was out and open to only a select group. Then a friend introduced me to psychologist and author Rob Eichberg, whose book, *Coming Out: An Act of Love*, was a bible to many people struggling to reveal their sexual orientation in the early 1990s. He encouraged me to come out but didn't shame me when I didn't act immediately. In 1991, I started working with David Mixner on Bill Clinton's presidential campaign. I was suddenly raising "gay dollars"—funds from LGBTQ donors from Mixner's network—for a political campaign. Previously these funds were not really welcomed, so this was an amazing cultural shift. As the unfamiliar governor of Arkansas started winning primaries and making headlines, there were also stories of Clinton's so-called gay money trail. I knew I had to confront my sexuality once and for all, especially with my family.

Rob had suggested that for many people, the best means of informing loved ones was by letter. His belief was that writing a letter, rather than standing in front of the recipient and waiting for a response, was perhaps fairer. As he put it, "You didn't deal with your sexuality overnight, so it isn't fair to feel they will. Give your family a chance to reflect."

It was the most difficult letter I ever wrote. I cried each time I read through it. But after months of equivocating, I sent it to my parents. This remains one of the most frightening times of my life. I wasn't afraid they wouldn't love or accept me; I was one of the lucky ones who knew my family would be there for me. But I still had the feeling I was letting them down. David Mixner knew I had sent the letter and checked in on me regularly. He had been through this experience himself years before and could relate.

My parents called as soon as they received the letter. My mom immediately told me that they loved me and not to worry. She expressed her concerns about how difficult it must have been during my school-age years to fear being "discovered" or to try to deny what I simply knew was true about myself. My dad was almost matter-of-fact, saying, "It's cool; we aren't in the dark ages." I know how lucky I am. I often think back to that frightened, ashamed little boy and think, *If he could only see that one day, I, an openly gay man, would be appointed to be special assistant to the president and social secretary—and it would be a positive press story.* I learned that in situations when you want to relay an important message, it's worth thinking carefully about the best way to be heard.

LOOK BETWEEN THE LINES

People with high emotional intelligence have the capacity to intuit the emotions of others and read their state of mind; they can then monitor their own feelings and behavior in order to manage relationships wisely. It's a bit like detective work: looking for nonverbal clues and then conducting yourself accordingly. We all read people to some degree, but training your powers of observation to be more focused and empathetic will pay generous dividends in friendship and good working relationships.

If you invite a colleague for lunch and she can't stop drumming the table and playing with the silver, perhaps she has a million things to do back at the office; maybe she had a fight with her spouse and she's agitated; maybe she's just overcaffeinated. A person with refined emotional intelligence skills might ask her about it gently or even cut the lunch short, making an excuse that it's time to get back to work, in order to let her go without prying.

During moments of silence, observe unspoken cues such as body position, eye contact, and what the speaker is doing with his hands and facial expression. Sometimes the most effective listening involves paying attention to what's *not* being said.

LEA

Deciding what a state dinner would look like was a delicate process because everyone had different ideas about what would be appropriate for the Indian president or the Australian prime minister (though the opinion that mattered most was Laura Bush's). The florist, Nancy Clarke, preferred more traditional bouquets. I always wanted unusual flowers in unique configurations; if I heard guests exclaiming over the flowers when they entered the dining room, I knew they were just right. Nancy and I would brainstorm three different floral arrangements, choose the china and tablecloths to go with them, and have the three tables set up in the room where the dinner was scheduled to take place.

The sample selection meetings were times when I made a point of reading Mrs. Bush's body language. Nobody wanted to hurt anyone's feelings, so the room would be very quiet, but I'd watch Mrs. Bush's facial expressions. If she quirked an eyebrow immediately, I knew she liked a table; if she rubbed the back of her neck with her hand, it was clear we were on the wrong track; and if she started changing plates or moving flowers to another table to see how it looked with a different cloth, I knew she had an idea of her own and was working it out. I would say something positive about the ones I could tell she liked to give Nancy a sense of where Mrs. Bush was headed. Reading those cues helped us work together easily without rejecting any of Nancy's hard work.

Other times you'll find that people *expect* you to read between the lines—what they mean is quite different from what they can or will openly say. The head of a well-known organization once asked the White House to host a dinner in honor of his group. He began the conversation by saying, "These White House parties are all so boring. How can we make them less boring?" It seemed like an odd way to ask for a favor, but there was a message beneath the request: he wanted a party at the White House the way a bride wants a swanky ballroom to impress her wedding guests. But he didn't like *us*, the Bush administration, and he wanted us to know it. However, the organization he represented was a worthy one, so we overlooked his not-so-subtle message in favor of supporting a good cause.

Every time there was an opportunity to cooperate across the political aisle, especially for a philanthropic purpose, we took it, because it gave us a chance to build connections with people and to show them we had more in common than they supposed.

THE FINE ART OF FUNNELING

Often the best way to broach a delicate conversation or a touchy subject is through a less difficult one. This can be thought of as funneling—beginning with a safe general topic and then proceeding carefully and diplomatically to the real issue. If you need to talk with a coworker about how much work he's been missing, it's best to start by asking him how his children are doing. There may be a legitimate reason for his absenteeism that he's been uncomfortable to talk about. If he assures you that all's well, this gives an opening to suggest that you thought perhaps something was wrong because he has been missing so much work. Rather than being openly critical and confrontational, you're showing that you're trying to be fair in considering a reason for the absences. This indirect approach can be a useful way to build alliances.

Our funneling skills were often called on in the White House calligraphy office. An average day in that office feels like a college library on the night before finals; everyone is working in a silent frenzy, addressing invitations, writing menus and place cards, or hand-lettering formal proclamations for the president. The calligraphers are perpetually behind, with too much work and never enough time to do it all. But they are artists of infinite imagination, painting lyrical watercolors of carousel ponies on the South Lawn for a picnic invitation or covering parchment menu cards with a script mimicking Shakespeare's handwriting for a dinner to celebrate the bard's birthday. Not all of their designs worked, but they were such creative, obliging people that we could never tell them outright if we didn't like their ideas. We would begin by reminding them of what a wonderful job they'd done on the last project, moving to what we liked about the current piece they were working on, and then gently suggesting a tweak here and there. It was the only respectful way to ask for changes without hurting feelings—and we couldn't bear to be unkind to them because we understood how hard they were working. Funneling is an effective and gentle way to get positive results.

THE OPEN-MINDED LISTENER

Listening well requires an open mind. Presidents often speak to friendly and supportive crowds, but there are also times when they must face less affable groups. No matter what the politics, it's important that the president be seen as truly hearing others who don't share his views. A president serves all the people, not just the ones who support him. Engaging with opponents to find areas where they can agree is an essential part of the job.

In 2006, President George W. Bush spoke at the NAACP Convention for the first time. He had turned down previous invitations because of the chairman's criticisms of him. But the Voting Rights Act was up for renewal, and the president determined that it was time to change the dynamic of the relationship. He spoke to the NAACP, knowing it would be a tough audience, and while he met with some boos and protests, the reception was generally polite. Any time you are able to reach out to communicate with those who have criticized you is a step in the right direction.

It's ironic that the Internet allows a massive volume of information to flow instantly around the world, yet we tend to use increasingly narrow channels for receiving information online. If you have a political point of view (and everyone does these days), do you ever really hear what the other side is saying? Many of us don't. We all need to become better listeners to different points of view.

The columnist Peter Wehner, senior fellow at the Ethics and Public Policy Center, writes frequently about the deepening polarization of American life and suggests that we should all engage in what Aristotle called "friendships of virtue." These friendships are based in mutual respect for the principles of another person, irrespective of her political beliefs. This happens less and less in Washington now, as members of Congress leave their families behind in their home districts instead of moving them to the capital. Neither they nor their spouses socialize with other members as they did when Washington was home base, and the across-the-aisle relationships that once proliferated and helped sustain bipartisanship have suffered. Friendship isn't meant to reinforce our personal opinions; a real friend, as Wehner writes, "elevates the sensibilities of the other, including from time to time helping us see things from a different angle."

It takes effort to keep these kinds of friendships going. We have to remind ourselves of the things that brought us together initially—our families, our community, or our shared love of country—to prevent political differences from poisoning our relationships.

One of the hardest things to take in is negative feedback, especially if it's coming from someone we don't like. Most people's initial reaction is to shut off anything or anyone they don't want to hear. It takes practice, but keeping an open mind during an unpleasant or combative conversation can help you see things from another point of view. It's a mark of maturity to put aside an emotional reaction and focus on the content of what's being said.

How do we do this? We hold our tongue (sometimes almost biting through it). We think about what we're going to say before we say it, and when we do speak, we soften our words to avoid open confrontation. Above all, we try to listen and grasp the other person's perspective. Tolerance of another person's viewpoint is the hallmark of a civil society.

We can't grow, or fix long-standing problems, if we listen only to the people with whom we already agree. We need to reclaim our individual right to draw our own conclusions by hearing the facts and making our own judgments. Don't be swayed by others when forming your opinions about a movie, an issue, or a person. That is your right and your obligation: to be a good listener is to be a good citizen.

We are still learning to listen ourselves. At the beginning of our collaboration for this book, we found that we were both being comically polite to each other as we talked around what we wanted to write about the White House. We gushed in our praise of the other's first lady. Jeremy would say kind things about a Republican president, and Lea would say something nice about a Democratic president. Our social secretary hypercourtesy was so ingrained that we each had to read between the lines of our conversations until we built enough trust to see that we had the same goal: sharing with others the techniques that helped us get along in the world more easily. Then we were able to be completely honest and offer helpful criticism to each other. Listening well, like all other important social skills, is a lifelong endeavor, and it's never too late to begin.

CHAPTER 5

Radiate Calm

Keep cool; anger is not an argument.

ANDREW JACKSON

S taying calm is assertive. When you remain serene, you're communicating that you have the situation under control and there's nothing to worry about. (Worrying won't change things anyway.) It's tempting to fly off the handle in a confrontational moment, but far more valuable to bring goodwill and order back to an unraveling situation. Maintaining a sense of equanimity even when matters are tense disarms antagonists, builds trust, and forces everyone involved to focus on the problem logically rather than emotionally, allowing for a better and quicker resolution.

Most people react to a crisis in the classic fight-or-flight response of the animal kingdom: they either shut down and become unable to move forward, or overreact and fling themselves into the fray, frantically doing everything they can think of in the panicky hope that something will work. We found that the best thing to do in those first precious seconds of a crisis is to adopt a coolly unflappable demeanor. Instead of running off or snapping back angrily, channel your energy into slowing down and putting on a game face. This may sound obvious, but people will be taking their cues from your reaction, so this will buy you a few moments to think about your options. Ask questions to be certain you understand as much about the situation as possible, and decide on a course of action only after you've had a moment to think things through. Being known as the steady hand on the rudder will allow you to build stronger support networks among your coworkers, and they will come to rely on your reasoned response and your ability to contain a problem.

We've identified four ways to radiate calm under any circumstances: stay composed, avoid drama, find common ground, and maintain perspective.

KEEP COOL

George Washington was a disciplined person who worked his entire life to control a fiery temper. Gilbert Stuart, the painter of the most famous image of Washington, the Lansdowne portrait that hangs in the East Room of the White House, once said that Washington's features "were indicative of the strongest and most ungovernable passions."

Washington recognized this quality in himself and made a lifelong effort to counteract it. As a sixteen-year-old, he copied "The Rules of Civility and Decent Behavior in Company and Conversation," based on a set of Jesuit precepts for the formation of good character. The 110 rules reflect heavily on the virtues of restraint, patience, and dignity. These lessons of his youth were invaluable during the Revolutionary War, when he contended with untrained troops, an absence of funds from the Continental Congress to feed or arm them, and constant wrangling with rivals over his role as commander of the army—punctuated by one military defeat after another. His longstanding efforts to remain sanguine helped prepare him for the crucial role he was to play in American history.

It takes self-discipline to convey calmness in your facial expressions and body language, but it can become second nature with time and practice. One of Jeremy's greatest natural skills is his quick wit; Lea's strength is her unflappability. If someone dropped a glass of red wine on the State Dining Room rug, she'd say, "We'll just get the salt," and sail off with a smile (even if inwardly she was thinking, *Not again!*). When an overzealous nun body-checked a female military aide in order to shake hands with President Bush on St. Patrick's Day, Lea made sure the aide was unhurt and then politely invited the slightly dazed nun into the dining room for something to eat. Almost everyone soon forgot the incident (though it's hard for Lea to erase the image of a habit-wearing elderly woman knocking a military officer to the floor).

In times of real crisis, it's even more essential to have control of your emotions. Calm, just like fear, is contagious. In 2015, one of the members of the White House press corps collapsed with a heart attack. The White House doctor on duty was called immediately (the White House Medical Unit serves the president and his family, but its five doctors are often brought in to treat guests or staff in an emergency). In the meantime, a Secret Service agent jumped in and efficiently performed CPR.

Those initial moments were chaotic and scary, but thanks to the swift, controlled work of the Secret Service, the Social Office, the military aides, and the ushers, no one panicked. We all understood how important it was to let the press corps and guests know that everything possible was being done on the reporter's behalf. It was a tremendous relief when the hospital informed us the next day that he was doing well; the Secret Service agent saved his life.

Both of the first ladies we worked for were experts in remaining unperturbed. (Barbara Bush once said, "Laura is the calm in George W.'s storm.") They never lost their cool, even in the trying moments that are a regular part of a first lady's day. Whether mobbed by a crowd of visiting tourists as they made their way to their office in the East Wing or forced to sit patiently with the wife of a head of state while painstakingly slow translations of small talk went on during an official visit, they each exhibited a steady poise that put others at ease.

LEA

The times when we most need to stay cool often occur when emotions are running high. I was wildly excited about my first Kennedy Center Honors reception, an annual event that celebrates five artists in recognition of their lifetime contribution to American culture. A standing-room-only black-tie reception at the White House precedes the show and draws more A-list star power than any other White House event. If the White House Correspondents' Association's annual dinner is Washington's "nerd prom," the Kennedy Center Honors reception is more like Oscar night.

As the reception was about to begin, I raced down the East Wing stairs and out a side door to the kitchen to avoid the crush of guests on their way to the State Floor. Wearing a black velvet strapless evening dress with a voluminous skirt and three looping strings of pearls, I pressed on the bar to open the door to the courtyard and swept outside, as I had a hundred times before, but my skirt got caught in the door. When I dashed ahead with full momentum, the slamming door jerked my dress down to my waist and there I was, stuck and topless, halfway out the service door to the White House kitchen. Thankfully, no one was there to see this, but I couldn't move. I tried to pull the top of my dress back up, but I couldn't stand without the dress being pulled down again by the weight of the door. Panicked, I thought about the security cameras, but couldn't decide if that was a good or a bad thing; if the Secret Service agents monitoring the area saw me, surely they would come and help—but then again, *What if the Secret Service agents saw me?* I took a deep breath, crouched down, and flung myself against the door like a crazed animal until it gave. I pulled my dress up into place, smoothed my hair, and took deep breaths as I continued to the State Floor. I began to feel reasonably collected. Then I took one step into the party and found myself face-to-face with Robert Redford, my girlhood movie crush. He gave me that half smile that makes women swoon, and I couldn't shake the feeling that he knew what had just happened (though that would have been impossible). "Good evening," I said to him and his wife, and quickly walked on. That was the most serenity I could manage under the circumstances.

On a more serious note, the combination of an unruffled demeanor and quick action can make all the difference when trying to achieve something in difficult or unexpected circumstances. On September 11, 2001, my fourteen-year-old daughter, Liddy, was in school when the planes hit the Twin Towers and she heard the false report that the White House had been attacked. She knew I was at work, so she quietly walked out of class, went to her younger sister's classroom, explained to several teachers that they were leaving, and took off toward our house, despite the fact that the entire school system was on lockdown. My husband found them walking home from school and told them I was safe.

We were all a little in awe of what Liddy had done, especially considering how worried she must have been about me.

When we questioned her about it later, she said, "I just thought we needed to be home." In the chaos of the day's events, her air of certainty caused every teacher she encountered to simply assume her departure had been approved. Acting with cool precision can help you appear powerful and in control, even if you might be roiling on the inside—and this holds true even if you are fourteen, in the midst of a terrorist attack.

JEREMY

Nothing hinted that Sunday, May 1, 2011, would be a memorable day. That afternoon I took a long walk to a party at the home of Fred Hochberg and Tom Healy. Fred was the chairman and president of the Export-Import Bank of the United States and had been appointed by the president. He and his partner, Tom, were famous for their dinner parties. Included that evening was a reporter from the *Washington Post* as well as one from the *New York Times*. The nine of us fit comfortably at the dinner table, but moments after taking my seat, I heard a BlackBerry buzzing. Then I realized it was mine, ringing from the pocket of my overcoat. The message said, "Close hold. POTUS to make statement from East Room tonight." The term *close hold* meant that I couldn't discuss it with anyone other than the White House staffers helping to execute the announcement. I walked over to Fred and whispered that I needed to leave, gathered my coat, and jumped into a cab. In the taxi, I said to myself, *Wow, everyone must be thinking: How incredibly rude of him—and that's the social secretary?*

The Social Office was responsible for making sure the ushers and essential staff were in place for the announcement. My deputy had already started contacting everyone and was on her way. As my cab made its way to the White House, I wondered with a mix of dread and excitement what had occurred to provoke the Sunday-evening remarks. (Weekends are not usually a time when a president addresses the nation unless it's something urgent, such as a threat to national security.)

After I arrived at the White House gate, the Secret Service told me there were rumors that Osama bin Laden had been found and either captured or killed. On the State Floor, staff were arranging the television camera setup and preparing for the historic announcement. As the National Security team arrived from the Situation Room and gathered in the Blue Room, President Obama walked to where I waited in the Green Room and calmly asked how I was doing. It was remarkable how composed he appeared, given the intense debates and decision-making that must have been occurring in the Situation Room all weekend, but he had also seemed at ease the night before as he tossed off funny remarks at the White House Correspondents' Association's annual dinner. Only a select few had any idea of the magnitude of what he was grappling with that evening.

Secretary Clinton, the vice president, CIA director Leon Panetta, deputy national security advisor Denis McDonough, chief of staff Bill Daley, and others on the security team entered the State Room to watch. I must have checked my two cell phones a dozen times to make sure they wouldn't start ringing as the leader of the free world addressed the nation with some of the most important news of the decade. Pete Souza photographed the group of us watching, which was all over the press and television immediately. I was standing in the back of the room, arms crossed, in a dark sweater (not in a suit as the others were, as my mother pointed out).

Around midnight, I received a message from Fred, my dinner party host. It simply said, "You're excused."

. . .

Even if you're not dealing with an international crisis, it can be hard not to panic in a charged situation. Here is our hard-won wisdom on how to coolly alleviate a high-pressure predicament:

Find your center. Take a few deep breaths. Then focus on understanding the situation and think quietly about your options.

Put people at ease. Ask questions, and soothe others around you who may be nervous. Don't hesitate to get a panicky person out of the way by sending him or her on an errand.

Shift into neutral. Keep your facial expression relaxed, your posture loose, and your voice soft and measured. But don't go overboard in appearing nonchalant: someone whose emotions are inflamed might view you as dismissive.

Make your move. Decide on a course of action. Then quickly begin to manage the situation before it can escalate. Speed is an ally in generating calm. It's how movie stars get through throngs of fans eager for photos and autographs: they move so swiftly that they're gone before almost anyone realizes they were there.

AVOID DRAMA

Drama makes for great reality television, but it's terrible for building strong relationships. Keeping your interactions with coworkers, family, and friends positive and light is crucial to gaining their confidence. If you explode in frustration every time there's a crisis, no one will look to you for a solution; instead, they will view you as part of the problem. Refusing to react to the frenzy establishes you as the adult in the situation who can be counted on to be helpful. Don't get angry; get things done.

It was an odd blessing that everything we did at the White House had the potential to become public. It made us think carefully about our actions, which almost always helped us find a considered response to sticky situations.

Rising calmly above such moments helped us to do our jobs successfully. At the most sought-after events, the headiness of being at a special party seemed to bring out a sort of manic energy in some people. We learned to turn the other cheek at rude behavior and outrageous demands. If a guest complained that an important friend of the president's had not been invited and that she intended to speak to the first lady about it, we would keep a measured tone and remind her that the first couple approves every guest. (You might be surprised to know that in the end, some guests do use their few seconds with the president and first lady to complain instead of saying something pleasant. What a missed opportunity!) If we seemed unconcerned about the person's threat, it gave her pause, and she reconsidered whether to gripe to the president and first lady. We worked every day to calmly distract and compliment our way out of those moments.

JEREMY

It was a rainy February afternoon, and President Obama was set to give a prestigious lifetime achievement award to a world-famous writer and humanitarian, along with other honorees, at the National Medal of the Arts and National Humanities Medal ceremony. A large and distinguished audience had gathered for the event, as had the White House press corps. Guests were mingling on the State Floor, the East Room was set with little gold opera chairs, and the podium with the presidential seal stood awaiting the arrival of the president. However, he was stuck in tense negotiations, and the ceremony was delayed, first a few minutes, then a few more. The writer bristled at being kept waiting, indignantly informing me that he had a plane to catch. At the time I was the White House liaison for the National Endowment for the Humanities and wouldn't become social secretary for another year, but social secretary Desirée Rogers and I went to work to soothe the honoree. Desirée offered to move his medal presentation to the beginning of the ceremony, and I tried to engage him in discussion on other topics.

The honoree repeatedly threatened to leave, so I stayed close to him, promising that the president would begin as soon as possible. The buffet reception normally reserved for after the ceremony was opened to guests, a musician from the president's Marine Band played the historic grand piano in the Grand Foyer, and most of the visitors were enjoying a little extra time to relax at the White House—but not our impatient writer. I might not have been on the job, but I recognized a public relations nightmare in the making when I saw one. No one had ever walked out on a White House medal ceremony without accepting the medal before.

As Daniel Shanks, an event usher since the Clinton administration, said, "This is a first, but we will just do our best." We were grateful that the other guests and honorees were having a great time, taking pictures, sitting in the Red Room, chatting and socializing. As soon as the president arrived, the ceremony began and the honoree was presented with his award—and then flew out the door in a huff. But the crisis was averted.

Often it isn't important to know why someone is behaving

in a certain way; what matters is how you respond. In this case, everyone worked calmly together to prevent an awkward situation from becoming a public embarrassment.

LEA

One sunny afternoon, as guests were arriving for a reception and moving through the Secret Service checkpoint, a woman wearing several long strands of seed pearls caught them on the clip of her purse and the necklace broke, sending hundreds of pearls in all directions. It was chaotic: the Secret Service officers could not leave their posts to help gather up the pearls that had scattered everywhere. The guest dropped to her knees and was trying to pick the pearls up, but the effort was taking a while. The other guests were getting annoyed with the delay, and the pearls were making people wobble and slide as they tried to walk over them. My assistant, Caroline Huddleston, was stationed at the gate and could see that things were moving out of control, so she held up her arms and called out, "If I could just get everyone's attention for a moment. This lovely lady has broken her pearl necklace. It would help her so much—well, really, it would help all of us—if you would pick up any of the pearls you see lying on the floor near you and give them to me as you pass through the magnetometers." Suddenly the disgruntled guests were bending over and scooping up pearls, smiling and joking. The pearls were gathered quickly because Caroline had the presence of mind to ask for everyone's help.

Drama begets drama. Here are some ways to reduce theatrics in work environments or social settings:

Recognize hot buttons. Try to keep people away from the volatile situations and subjects that set them off. If a holiday volunteer hyperventilated each time she saw the president or first lady, we would assign her to be anywhere *except* near them. If you know your best friend has a pet peeve about being kept waiting, don't be late. If someone likes stirring the pot and can't respect opinions that differ from his own, think carefully about including him in gatherings with people of varied views.

Nip hysteria in the bud. Some people carry drama with them wherever they go. Ignoring the histrionics is like depriving a fire of oxygen. Rumors also breed drama, so knock them down as swiftly as possible; this gives gossips nowhere to go, and keeps your reaction from becoming part of the story.

Don't escalate. Take what people are saying at face value and act on the facts you know, not the emotions you may feel. Anyone feeding into a conflict by spreading inaccurate information or getting worked up is only making things worse.

Temper your tone. There's a saying that applies particularly well in Washington: "Always keep your words soft and sweet, in case you have to eat them." Whenever you find yourself in a charged situation, try to deliver your comments in a positive—or at least neutral—tone. There will probably be a few times when you wish you had voiced your anger more forcefully, but more often we wish we'd said less.

Go to the source. One of the first lessons we learned at the White House was to make sure we were acting on accurate information rather than relying on hearsay. Occasionally an acquaintance of the first lady would call and say, "The first lady told me to tell you to invite my brother-in-law/secretary/high school basketball team/hair stylist to a party. Here's their address and phone number." They hoped we would be too busy to check, but as Ronald Reagan said in his talks with Mikhail Gorbachev, "Trust, but verify."

FIND COMMON GROUND

Sometimes we have to deal with problems that aren't of our own making but nevertheless affect our ability to be successful. Don't shy away from becoming an intermediary between two parties in conflict if you can help them arrive at a resolution. You may feel trapped at first, but remember that if you treat both sides with equal respect and honesty and have an investment in the outcome, this is a position of influence. Being open to multiple paths to a solution also allows you to approach all kinds of dilemmas creatively.

LEA

One of the jobs of the chief usher is to protect and maintain the White House as a museum of American presidential history. One of the tasks of the White House communications staff is to make the White House look beautiful and majestic when seen on television. These two assignments were often in conflict, causing some angry disagreements. Gary Walters, the chief usher, and Scott Sforza, the communications staffer whose job it was to create memorable backdrops for all televised events, clashed about many things: whether the presidential podium for a joint press conference with a foreign leader looked best on the East Room's east or west wall, or which rooms could be used for filming public service announcements, for example. An explosive confrontation came when one of the communications staff assistants innocently moved a rare mantel clock in the Red Room to set up a television shot, not knowing it was a historic antique that no one except the White House curator or the clock winder ever touched. (Yes, there was once a White House clock winder. There's been a tradition of several generations of families serving as White House employees from the earliest days, although now the clocks are wound by the White House electricians.)

After the clock incident, a cold war raged between the two men, and their dislike for each other grew into a continuing problem. I understood their differing points of view and was increasingly drawn into their disagreements as the impartial third party. To their credit, they saw the value of an informal arbiter and found a way to get along through me.

Gary would come to me and say, "Can you tell Scott that we can't get any more flags in the Grand Foyer for the press conference? They're using the extra flags at an event in the Eisenhower building today." Scott would accept that reason from me more easily than he would from Gary. By helping them reach common ground and "making them both right," I found consensus. As a result, events ran more smoothly—which was, in the end, the whole idea.

JEREMY

In December, shortly after the 2012 election, Mrs. Obama gathered her staff for a series of planning retreats in the Eisenhower Executive Office Building for several Saturday mornings and some afternoons. The goal was to get everyone's ideas and strategize for the next four years of the administration. Staff

Lea checking the seating before a 2005 dinner in honor of Prince Charles and his new wife, Camilla, duchess of Cornwall. The charger plates were part of the Clinton china—social secretaries are bipartisan when it comes to an event's decor.

From *left*: Blake Gottesman, President Bush's personal aide; Deputy Social Secretary Missy DeCamp; and Lea, dining in the Usher's Office during the prince of Wales and the duchess of Cornwall dinner.

Considering tablescapes in the China Room, where samples of presidential china dating back to the Monroe administration are on display. From *left*: White House florist Nancy Clarke, Mrs. Bush, Lea, Anita McBride, and White House curator William Allman.

Lea greeting President Clinton on one of his many visits to the Bush White House.

The cast of *Jersey Boys* perform in the East Room for the 2006 Senate Spouses' Luncheon, with Mrs. Bush looking on. Lea had booked them months in advance, not knowing that the show would win the Tony for Best Musical the night before.

Lea, accompanied by her daughter Alice, then fourteen, receiving an honor guard from the White House social aides upon arriving at her farewell dinner with the Bushes, 2007.

Lea and the first lady sharing a moment in the family quarters during that same farewell dinner.

President George W. Bush with Lea's daughters, Liddy and Alice, at the postwedding brunch for Amy Allman Dean, the director of the White House Visitors Office, at the Bushes' home in Dallas, 2010.

Jeremy and President Obama in the Oval Office in May 2015 going over the guest list of an unofficial party at which Prince would perform.

Jeremy walking the Obamas to the elevator up to the residence at the end of the National Governors Gala, an annual bipartisan White House event. Mrs. Obama presented the 2014 Academy Award for Best Picture later that evening.

Pete Souza / The White House

Christmas in July! It was always a challenge to get in the holiday spirit when presenting the decor in the middle of the summer. Here, the social office staff and florist review options with the first lady in 2012.

Pete Souza / The White House

Jeremy placing the official White House Historical Association ornament on a tree in the Diplomatic Reception Room.

Courtesy of Lea Berman

Please respond to
The Social Secretary
The White House
at your earliest convenience
giving full name (first, middle, and last),
gender, date of birth, social security number,
city and state of residence, and country of birth

(202)
Social Office R S V P

The traditional RSVP card sent in all White House invitations. These days, it's included as an email attachment.

Jeremy dressed as a character from *Men in Black* in the Blue Room with President and Mrs. Obama, about to greet military families picnicking on the South Lawn.

Jeremy wears one of the hats created for the 2014 Kids' State Dinner as POTUS stops by to say hello. Once an event is under way, it becomes easier to relax and enjoy the festivities.

Jeremy jokes with President and Mrs. Obama and White House press secretary Jay Carney at a reception for the second inauguration in January 2013.

The president and first lady dancing with Jeremy at the going-away party they hosted for him in 2015. President Obama asked guests to put their cameras away so that he and Jeremy could do one last "Jeremy dance."

Hosted by Deesha Dyer, the 2016 Christmas lunch at the White House with the former social secretaries took place in the Vermeil Room, where many of the first ladies' portraits can be found—Grace Coolidge's portrait is in the background. From *left* to *right*: Lea Berman, Cathy Fenton, Julianna Smoot, Jeremy Bernard, Ann Stock, Amy Zantzinger, Bess Abell, Gahl Hodges Burt, and Deesha Dyer.

members researched what previous first ladies had done—what worked and what did not work so well. (One historic lesson was to have multiple initiatives—but not too many.) The workshops took place in various ornate rooms.

The staff members were divided into teams that reported on different topics, and Mrs. Obama attended as a team member as well. She didn't have her hair and makeup done as she did for events in front of the public. She made it very easy to consider her one of us. These retreats provided the first lady's agenda for the next term but also built consensus because each member felt involved.

An opportunity for me to practice my own skills at consensus building came in late July 2011. The occasion was a senior staff meeting for long-term schedule planning, the last item on Mrs. Obama's calendar before she left for summer break. Each department (Social, Communications, Policy and Initiatives) had come armed with a presentation for the coming year. The meeting dragged on for several hours. We finally got to discuss holiday parties and the theme for the year, a difficult topic on a hot summer afternoon. A great deal of thought and care goes into deciding these holiday themes, which the Communications Office and the General Counsel's Office review. It always seemed like much ado about nothing, but everything was carefully scrutinized on the assumption that if someone in the press could find a way to turn a simple holiday theme into something problematic, he or she would. We had previously suggested "Shine Forth," which the Communications Office rejected. We had now come up with "Shine, Give, Share" as the holiday theme, and Mrs. Obama had approved it.

When the long afternoon of meetings was finally over, I went to the door of Mrs. Obama's office, revealing a surprise. The social staff, social interns, chef, and calligraphers came in with trays full of holiday cookies and glasses of champagne. This small preview of the holiday reception thrilled Mrs. Obama and was welcomed by everyone, ending a tough afternoon of meetings on a positive note. The small effort inspired people to work together and achieve consensus when it came to the rest of the holiday planning.

Creating consensus is an important part of staying composed. If you know how to get people to sit down at the table and agree on things, you can accomplish almost anything. Here are a few tips for bringing people together in a calm and productive way:

Open the floor. Include all participants in the decision-making process, especially if the group is small. Allow everyone to discuss the situation frankly. In this way, all will be invested in the outcome.

Create options. Generate as many choices as possible from the largest number of people. You may end up deciding on something that doesn't please everyone, but at least staffers will feel that their ideas have been heard. And you'll be surprised by how often a productive brainstorming session leads to a breakthrough on another issue.

Reset as needed. If you get to an impasse, return to basics. Find one small thing, however trivial, on which the group agrees, and remind them of it. It could be something as unimportant as where you order out for lunch that day. Take a break and talk about something else—sports, movies, anything that helps people see each other as colleagues rather than opponents. This will ease tensions and eventually get everyone back to finding a solution.

MAINTAIN PERSPECTIVE

Most of the things we worry about never happen, and many of the things that keep us up at night are beyond our control. For situations we can fix or ameliorate, it's crucial to keep their relative importance in perspective. You don't want to get hysterical over whether the first lady will like the Christmas party invitation designs, and you don't want to be blithe about a life-or-death matter. Having perspective is an essential part of staying calm and effective; when you understand the weight of a task, you'll be more likely to apply the right amount of effort.

In 1955, when President Eisenhower was scheduled to speak at the Penn State commencement ceremonies, officials (including his brother, who was president of the university) worried that threatening weather would mar the ceremony, and they asked him if they should move the proceedings indoors.

"You decide," he said. "I haven't worried about the weather since June 6, 1944." When you've planned the greatest invasion of all time—the day Allied forces stormed the beaches of Normandy, France, to fight the Nazis in World War II—it's hard to care very much about a little rain. Perspective reminds us of what really matters.

LEA

When I started as social secretary, I had an unhealthy, fearful attitude toward the job. I couldn't see that I had created unrealistic expectations, striving for perfection and twisting myself into knots of worry over every tiny detail. After a particularly trying day, I put my head down on my desk and fought back tears, thinking,

What have I gotten myself into? At that exact moment, the phone rang. It was Ann Stock, who had been social secretary to Bill and Hillary Clinton for five years, offering to host a luncheon so I could meet the other former White House social secretaries.

It was one of the most valuable afternoons of my life and came at precisely the moment I needed it most. Each of these resourceful, vibrant women had conquered the White House; they had negotiated political tempests, cleaned up other people's messes, made historic moments happen, prevented bad ideas from going forward, and ultimately prevailed with great success. They were living proof of facing the challenges of the job, surmounting them, and thriving while doing it. Hailing from the Kennedy, Johnson, Ford, Reagan, Clinton, Bush 41, and Bush 43 administrations, these extraordinary women were completely honest, welcoming, and full of hilarious off-the-record stories. They told me about their disasters and near misses and how they dealt with famously difficult people. They gave me the gift of perspective.

I left that luncheon with a fresh, positive attitude about my ability to succeed. I love these women and will never forget how much they helped me. The tradition of welcoming new social secretaries continues as we try to be a resource for the current social secretary, and I hope we continue to give the benefit of our experience to each new member of what we refer to as "the sorority and Jeremy."

Here's some advice about how to keep the right perspective:

You can't control everything. If your plane is delayed and you're about to miss an important business meeting, don't blame the airline personnel. Arrange a conference call so you can take part in the meeting. If that's impossible, dash off an explanation and start making a list of follow-up questions. You'll be focusing on what you can do rather than obsessing about what you can't.

Set your priorities. Remind yourself of what's truly important to you, and don't confuse other people's inclinations and interests with your own. Examine your expectations with a critical eye. Are they unrealistic? Have you scheduled too short a time line for a complicated task? If so, give yourself a break.

Appreciate where you are. There's nothing like a daily review of your advantages and blessings to remember the big picture. Reach out to others who have been in your shoes. This will also give you a glimpse of the long view.

There's a reason the British World War II expression "Keep Calm and Carry On" resonates on mugs, towels, and postcards: the message is reassuring and uplifting. Who doesn't like to be calmed down *and* lifted up? Now that you know how, you'll notice that radiating calm in heated moments and in daily life changes the way you feel. And because it conveys maturity and competence, it also changes how others see you.

CHAPTER 6

Handle Conflict Diplomatically

Civilization is a method of living,
an attitude of equal respect for all men.

Jane Addams

R esolving conflicts deftly takes an open, positive outlook and a mastery of the people skills we've already discussed: confidence, charm, careful listening, and a calm demeanor. A disagreement doesn't have to be a terrible experience that ends in a stressful confrontation; sometimes it's a path to improvement. People who treat others well don't stonewall or criticize; instead, they collaborate, seize opportunities, and try to create a better result for everyone concerned.

Before you enter a conflict, you first have to know what you are willing to give up and what you aren't. Resolving a disagreement is not a zero-sum game, and total domination is not the point. If you can look after your own interests while maintaining an awareness of your opponent's needs, you may be able to find workable solutions that form the basis for a stronger, more productive relationship going forward.

Sometimes the best way to handle a conflict is by refusing to engage before it even starts. When the Berlin Wall fell in 1989, signaling the beginning of the end of the Soviet Union, President

George H. W. Bush's advisors suggested he go to Germany to celebrate the end of decades of a divided Germany. His response was: "What would I do? Dance on the wall?" His restraint as events in Germany and the Soviet Union unfolded prevented hard-liners in the Soviet government from stirring up anger and resentment against the United States into aggressive action and gave reformers like Mikhail Gorbachev time to manage the transition to a peaceful end to the Soviet Union.

The Camp David Accords signed in 1978 between two long-standing adversaries, Egypt and Israel, were an example of Jimmy Carter's skill at conflict resolution. President Carter kept Menachem Begin and Anwar Sadat negotiating at Camp David for nearly two weeks. Just when it seemed the talks had collapsed, Carter was able to persuade the two leaders to make concessions that led to their historic agreement and the Nobel Peace Prize for both of them. Carter helped Begin and Sadat find their common interest on an intractable issue. His ability to see the possibilities, and not just the obstacles, made this diplomatic breakthrough possible.

We found that in all kinds of scenarios, there were three tactics we could rely on to resolve conflicts effectively: engage with the problem, establish boundaries, and control your response.

FACE THE MUSIC

It's only human to want to avoid a battle, but the faster you move in to engage with a problem, the faster you can navigate out of it. Instead of thinking, "What went wrong?" ask yourself, "How are we going to fix this?" Failure to act promptly allows tensions to fester and magnify. And if a dispute or situation is unfolding rapidly, sometimes it's best to tackle it yourself—even if you didn't cause it.

LEA

One of the first events I planned at the White House was an annual tea that Laura Bush hosted for a venerable women's service organization. We were expecting three hundred and fifty guests, who were to arrive on buses for a reception with the first lady: no speeches, no program—just tea and dainty sweets. It should have been straightforward, but things soon began to unravel. One of the buses hit the steel gates of the southeast entrance to the White House as it rolled into East Executive Drive and the gates froze, stuck on "open."

Meanwhile, a group of women who had already arrived in another bus were waiting in line outside the White House. As one of the guests showed her ID, two agents stepped up and began to read her her rights. Then they arrested, handcuffed, and marched her off (though they did fold her coat over her handcuffs in an effort to be discreet). Her companions, assuming a terrible injustice had been done, pulled out their cell phones and began bombarding their senator's office with outraged calls. The senator immediately called both the White House Office of Legislative Affairs and the Oval Office to demand that his constituent be released. The first I heard of all this was a call from Blake Gottesman, President Bush's personal aide.

"Was someone arrested at your tea party?" he asked gently. "Because a senator just called to complain to the president about it."

"A guest was arrested?" I gasped. "The *president* knows about this?"

"Not yet," Blake said. "Can you help?"

Then the less polite calls from the Legislative Affairs Office started: they were also hearing plenty from the angry senator. This is known in Social Office parlance as a "pearl-clutching moment." I could feel the blood rushing to my face. It wasn't ideal that the president might hear about the arrest, but I was far more worried that the press would get wind of it. This was exactly the kind of story that could become fodder for late-night talk show hosts.

I could have lost my temper with the Secret Service agents, and it might have felt good in the moment. But the agent in charge of the event was a person I respected and trusted, so I called him from the State Floor, where the tea had already started. He told me the woman in question had several outstanding federal bench warrants, and the Secret Service was obliged to arrest her if she tried to enter a federal facility. They knew from our clearance lists that she had accepted the invitation and were waiting for her. In other words, it was no mistake.

Once I understood this, the path forward was clear. One of the agents took the woman's friends aside and explained the situation; they were stunned. Even the senator's aides apologized to our staff, saying they had reacted rashly. The problem was settled within fifteen minutes—and it wasn't brought to the president's attention until *after* it was resolved.

But the excitement wasn't over. Minutes later I heard shouts coming from the Green Room, where guests were lining up for their photos with the first lady. I rushed in to find a gaggle of women arguing so boisterously that I thought Mrs. Bush must be able to hear them from upstairs. I introduced myself and asked if I could be of help. The disagreement seemed to be over who would be first in the photo line.

I said loudly, in my best mother-in-charge voice, "Ladies, there will be no pictures for *anyone* today if you don't stop shouting."

This was a bluff, but I had their attention. "Mrs. Bush is going to be here any moment. Would you want her to see you behaving this way?" Chastened, they rearranged themselves into a line, glaring and grumbling, but the rest of the event went by without incident. It may not have been our smoothest party, but we managed to resolve these conflicts swiftly enough to prevent any real damage or embarrassment. (Note to felons: if you're invited to the White House, you may not get the reception you expect.)

Here are some things to remember when you need to act fast:

Get your facts straight. If Lea had not gotten a speedy explanation from various people around the White House about what had occurred at the gate that spring afternoon, the story would have taken on a life of its own and her reputation would have taken a hit. Ask questions that help you understand the situation: What happened? Who's involved? How can we stop it? Is there anything you're not telling me? How much time do we have to fix it?

Step in. When something needs to be taken care of, you shouldn't worry about people thinking you might be too aggressive. Lea didn't worry about her tone when a bill signing scheduled for the South Lawn was interrupted by a vote in the House of Representatives. Suddenly, eighty out of one hundred members of Congress who were gathered on the lawn, waiting for their photo op with President Bush, abruptly left to go vote. The president was already striding across the grass, and a background of empty chairs was not the strongest political message to send. Lea raced over with two staffers and began pulling chairs as fast as they could, asking the twenty remaining members to fill the space behind where the president would be seated. The last chair was dragged off the risers just as he arrived, and the final photo featured a background of members smiling behind the president, their support preserved for posterity. Lea and her staffers limped back across the lawn (heels ruined by the grass), soaked in perspiration but relieved.

Provide updates. If there's time and the situation is not confidential, let your colleagues know you're aware of the problem and working on it. There is no need to go into detail, but they will appreciate being kept in the loop.

Sometimes conflicts can be anticipated, as when you're invited to sit down to a negotiation. When that happens, remember that most people we disagree with are not our enemies. If you head into deliberations with the sole goal of eviscerating the other party, you're virtually ensuring that the dispute will escalate.

Remind yourself that dissent can be a path to progress, particularly if you're committed to being collaborative. Ronald Reagan kept a plaque in his office with a famous Harry S. Truman quote on it: "There is no limit to the amount of good you can do if you don't care who gets the credit."

Here are some guidelines for negotiating effectively.

Acknowledge the opposition. Remind yourself that the person you're crossing swords with has a different but equally valid point of view. Try to see the problem from his perspective, just as you hope he would do for you.

Be assertive and clear. Communicate your needs firmly, not aggressively. When emotions are running high, try to remember that conflict is an opportunity for growth: as you work through a problem with another person, your relationship becomes stronger.

Use inclusive words. Choose *we* and not *I*, as in, "How are *we* going to solve this problem?" "What if *we* try another way?" Collaboration is better than combat when you're trying to get something done.

Recognize alternatives. Don't ignore objections. Listening to others makes participants feel heard and keeps the conversation moving forward.

GOOD FENCES MAKE GOOD NEIGHBORS, COLLEAGUES, AND FRIENDS

An enormously helpful way to ease a dispute—or prevent one in the first place—is to establish boundaries. Make yours clear while recognizing those of others. If you know your limits and communicate them directly, people may not like what you're saying, but they'll know where you stand and respect your commitment to your beliefs. Boundaries inspire order.

If your coworker makes a practice of showing up at meetings to which he's not invited, take him aside and explain that the meetings are limited in number for a reason. This is a reminder that he's overstepped the mark. Then ask if there's specific information he feels he's missing. You'll likely get a useful answer instead of a repeat of the unwanted behavior.

Whenever you can, invoke preexisting standards. This can give your position a sense of weight and history. In the White House, we frequently let others we worked with know what was required, what was negotiable, and what wasn't even worth asking about. We used long-established traditions as a shield to ward off inappropriate requests from guests. *We* weren't saying no, and guests couldn't really get upset with *the White House.*

JEREMY

Once, on a visit to the Obamas, a CEO arrived at Dulles Airport on his private jet and phoned me to say he was concerned that traffic would cause him to be late for his appointment. He suggested that he charter a helicopter to fly into Washington if I could secure clearance for him to land on the South Lawn. I explained that only the president had that privilege. Not even the vice president or the first lady—and certainly no one else—could arrive in such a manner. (After President Reagan was shot in 1981, Vice President George H. W. Bush actually refused to have the helicopter take him directly to the White House because he wanted to respect that honor.) After I calmly explained the White House protocol of helicopter arrivals on the South Lawn, he realized his plea wasn't realistic and dropped it—and arrived in plenty of time via limousine.

LEA

When I first came to the White House, I did a terrible job of defending my boundaries. It was so ingrained in me to be accommodating, to keep things running smoothly at all costs, that suppressing my feelings over professional altercations eventually took its toll on my emotional well-being. I came to realize that if I didn't give myself the same respect I accorded to others, no one else would either.

There was a staffer around the residence who loved to offer her opinions about all kinds of things, even in areas that had no bearing on her own duties. I didn't speak up when she inserted herself into issues that should have been of no concern to her because she seemed harmless enough and I wanted (too much) to keep things collegial.

Assembling the dress rehearsal buffet for the holiday parties, practice for how the table would look, was the culmination of weeks of effort by the chefs, the florists, and the Social Office. One time I was standing by the dessert table, discussing the arrangement with Bill Yosses, the pastry chef, and I placed a big trifle bowl at one end of the table. The staffer in question came up behind me and said, "That doesn't work there at all. It needs to go here," and she moved it to the center of the table. When Mrs. Bush came down to look at the buffet, she walked around the State Dining Room, admiring the decorations and making small suggestions. When she came to the dessert buffet, she looked at the trifle bowl, picked it up, and moved it back to where I had originally placed it. The woman turned to me and said, in front of Mrs. Bush, "I told you not to put the trifle bowl in the middle of the table. It looks so much better there."

I couldn't believe she'd done that—and over something so small—but I held my fire and said nothing. If I had corrected her in front of Mrs. Bush, I would have seemed like the petty one, not her. But that doesn't mean I shouldn't have said something later. To be fair, how could she know she was driving others crazy when none of us had the courage to tell her?

I finally hit my limit when she walked into my office one day, looked at a set of four prints hanging on the wall, and observed that they were "too feminine" and needed to be replaced. This time I looked at her calmly and said, "My husband bought me those prints to hang in this office."

A look of panic flitted across her face, and she literally backed out of my office without saying another word. I had finally let her know that she'd gone too far, and we never had another issue.

Here are some suggestions for using boundaries to avoid conflict:

Set limits. Don't let your fear of confrontation allow others to trample them. If you don't want to be texted on Sunday nights about work matters, be firm that this time is off-limits, and don't answer any texts during that time unless it's an emergency. If a colleague likes to drop by on Monday mornings and rehash the weekend, it is reasonable to keep your chat to a minimum so that you can get started on the day. If you want to be off the grid during a vacation, write a memo to your coworkers explaining the dates that you will be unavailable and which person to contact if there is a pressing issue.

Keep fast to them. Don't be intimidated into violating your personal line in the sand. Peer pressure is not just for kids; throughout our lives, we're pushed to behave in ways that make us uncomfortable. The earlier we learn to ignore those pressures, the easier it is to stay true to ourselves.

Don't tolerate harassment of any kind. It should be a given by now that lewd comments or gestures and overfamiliar observations about others' physical appearances are inappropriate. If you see unprofessional behavior of that nature—or are the subject of it—don't ignore it: take the appropriate steps to see that it is addressed.

Use common sense. Don't overshare personal information or unconfirmed rumors, especially in a work setting. Politely change the subject if someone infringes on your privacy with an untoward question. Recognize unspoken rules to prevent tensions from escalating. Don't take an extra-long lunch break during a crunch time. If you have to be out of the office on a busy day, make arrangements to stay late the night before or come in early to do your share. By observing obvious work boundaries, you encourage others to do the same.

MODULATE YOUR RESPONSE

Thinking through your comments and actions while embroiled in a dispute will prevent you from saying something so terrible that it can never be forgiven. Words that spill out in a moment of unchecked anger can change a relationship forever. Try to separate a specific disagreement with a person from your attitude toward that person.

Feelings of resentment or the desire to retaliate make conflict resolution more difficult. Avoid sarcasm, contempt, criticism, and defensiveness in dealing with a problem; they only inflame the situation and harden your opponent's position. Before you lose your temper, remind yourself of the larger goal to be gained.

JEREMY

There are times when we just need to button our lip, as hard as it might be. I was a guest at a dinner party one cold January evening. I knew only the host, so I made a point of introducing myself as I made my way through the lavish living room. Standing in front of the fireplace was a young man looking at the various photographs on the mantel. I asked how long he had known the host (always a reliable opening line), and he started recounting how they met at "one of those god-awful White House holiday receptions." He spoke of how bored he got hanging out in all those "old rooms as everyone took photos." At first I wondered if he was joking because he jumped into it so quickly, but it was soon apparent that he was serious. I literally bit my tongue as I continued listening, a smile frozen on my face.

Later, as we were all seated at a dinner table that seemed almost as vast as the one in the State Dining Room of the White House, the host briefly commented about each one of his guests, ensuring we all had a chance to get to know one another. Out of the corner of my eye, I saw the reaction of the young man as our host said, "And we are lucky that Jeremy Bernard, the White House social secretary, has the night off and could join us here tonight." The young man's jaw dropped for a moment, and he whispered something to the person next to him. Later, as I was departing, I made a point of shaking his hand and expressing how nice it was to meet him. He apologized for his gaffe. I brushed it aside with a laugh, saying, "No worries."

This became a favorite story for my staff, and at our morning meetings, as we discussed the previous day's activities, they often joked that it was "just another one of those god-awful events," meaning everything had gone well.

Instead of acting out, recognize that most conflicts are short-lived and find a healthy outlet for your anger and frustration. On a particularly trying day, Jeremy would ask that his assistant give him five minutes with no interruptions and shut the door. Once the door clicked closed, he would sit away from his desk and briefly meditate, a few minutes of tranquility that yielded enormous stress-relieving benefits. After a tough day at the White House, Lea used to turn up the radio in her car and sing along to the loudest, happiest music she could find. By the time she got home, she felt much better and was able to relax with her family without taking her work frustrations out on them.

We are indebted to our White House experience for helping us learn to resolve disputes speedily, establish our own personal and professional boundaries, and respect those of others. Behaving as if we live in the public eye means responding with restraint and thoughtfulness when faced with challenging situations.

Conflict resolution is a lifelong skill that begins in childhood. When kids see parents and caregivers negotiating positively, they will form a habit of settling disputes reasonably. They will learn to stand up for themselves while regulating their emotions, a helpful tool in resisting peer pressure. This is an extraordinary gift and, like so many of the other aspects of treating people well, eminently teachable.

CHAPTER 7

Honesty Is the Best Policy
(Except When It Isn't)

✧ ✧ ✧

Truth is powerful and it prevails.

SOJOURNER TRUTH

A mong the presidents considered to have been the most honest, Grover Cleveland is not a name that immediately leaps to mind. He's mostly known as the only president to serve two nonconsecutive terms and for fathering a child out of wedlock. Yet Cleveland's straight-arrow reputation and fight against corruption propelled him from mayor of Buffalo to governor of New York, where he successfully challenged the entrenched forces of Tammany Hall, and then all the way to the presidency. Publisher Joseph Pulitzer's endorsement listed four reasons why people should vote for Cleveland: "1) He is honest. 2) He is honest. 3) He is honest. And 4) He is honest."

When it emerged, just before the 1884 presidential election, that Cleveland had a son born out of wedlock, the unmarried Cleveland acknowledged his relationship with the mother and admitted that he supported the child. It may be the only sex scandal that ever *helped* a candidate: Cleveland became the first Democrat to win the White House in more than thirty years.

Honesty is a trait we all admire, but it takes tact to be forthright. You'll need to have some level of comfort with confidence, calmness, and handling conflict in order to know how to share a difficult truth, or when to leave out a piece of information that serves no useful purpose other than to hurt the listener.

The first thing you need to know is that although truth is always preferable, a lie can be loving and gentle. And telling the truth can sometimes be cruel and pointless. We pride ourselves on being aboveboard, but we've found there are times when the most appropriate action is to skirt delicately around the truth.

Three essential concepts guided us when it came to candor: be up front whenever possible, know when a truth will help or harm, and take the long view.

START BY COMING CLEAN

Sometimes you might be tempted to hide a fact you are embarrassed about, especially in situations like a job interview. But being truthful in that setting is a refreshing way of establishing yourself as a person of integrity. When Muffie Brandon met with President Reagan to interview for the position of social secretary, one of the first things she did was remind him that she was a registered Democrat. According to Muffie, he replied, "*I* used to be a Democrat. What we're looking for are the best people to serve our country." Their mutual candor set the tone for a great working relationship.

JEREMY

I was working at the US Embassy in Paris when I got an email from someone who worked for Mrs. Obama, inquiring if I would be interested in throwing my hat in the ring for the social secretary position because Julianna Smoot would be leaving to work on the reelection campaign. I didn't think twice. I arrived in DC the weekend before the interview to buffer any possible travel delays and to adjust to the time change (remember: preparation builds confidence). After a morning of meetings with individual senior staff members, I was escorted to Mrs. Obama's East Wing office. She hugged me, and we spoke about Paris for a moment before getting down to business. I started with a disclaimer that I feared was problematic, but I wanted to be honest. "I must admit I'm far from an expert with flowers, and I don't know linens," I said. She laughed, and told me that there were others on the staff who had opinions about both. After the interview, I told Julianna about my opening comment and she laughed too, saying she had confessed to Mrs. Obama virtually the same thing when she was interviewed. (And both of us were hired.)

I attribute my reliance on telling the truth to an incident that happened when I was in high school in Texas. Three of my friends and I broke the rules and left to have lunch off-campus. Not long after, we were called to the office of the headmaster, Reverend Daunt. Before we could collaborate on our stories, we were interrogated, one by one. The others stumbled; one said she was trying to sell ad space for the yearbook. When it was my turn, I threw my hands in the air and said that I just "wanted to go have lunch somewhere other than here." Reverend Daunt chuckled, and we were sent back to class, unpunished.

LEA

In the summer of 1987, George H. W. sent his son George W. Bush, along with my husband, to meet with Rep. Ed Madigan to seek his endorsement for the Republican nomination. Madigan's response was less than promising. He said to George W. Bush, "When I had a primary as a sitting member of Congress, I asked your father for help and no one from his staff ever called me back. So why do you think I'd want to lead the charge for him now?"

George W. Bush responded, "On behalf of my father, I'm very sorry no one on his staff ever called you back. That's not how my father operates. He's a true gentleman, and I know he'd be really angry if he knew about this. Of course, I don't expect you to endorse, but I want you to know that we'd like your support, and I want you to have my phone number. If you ever need anything from me, the campaign, or my dad, you can call me, and I'll always take your call."

Two days later, Madigan endorsed George H. W. Bush for president, telling my husband, Wayne, that his conversation with George W. Bush "was the most honest interaction I've ever had with anyone in Washington." With his sincerity, Bush turned an opponent into a supporter. And the relationship grew from there: Madigan was eventually appointed George W. Bush's secretary of agriculture.

The truth is, being dishonest in the working world can be dangerously entangling; the smallest fabrication can call your reputation into question. Be clear about your capabilities. Don't tell your boss you can speak Spanish fluently if your learning experience consists of two years in middle school. When you're asked to give a new Spanish-speaking client a tour of the office, your dishonesty will be revealed in a particularly embarrassing way.

Another important rule of thumb is not to promise anything you can't deliver. As much as political supporters love to host a candidate, they sometimes overlook the fact that their homes don't have the capacity to support a presidential-style event. On one occasion at a fundraiser's country home, the promised "ample parking" turned out to be a rough field nearby. As the rainy evening wore on, more than a hundred cars began to sink past their hubcaps into the waterlogged grass. An alert event planner, Lindsay Reynolds, saw what was happening, called every tow truck in a forty-mile radius, and immediately began having the cars towed out of the field. By the time dinner was over, the guests' cars had been pulled from the muck and were lined up along the drive, muddy but accessible. Guests never knew the disaster that Lindsay prevented, but you can be sure people thought twice before planning any political events at that home again.

KNOW WHEN TO SHARE OR SHELTER THE TRUTH

We know we should tell the truth whenever possible, but sometimes a fib spares someone else's feelings while reinforcing your regard for him or her. Lea's mother-in-law, Sally, was a terrible cook. At the end of the day, as Sally began to putter around the kitchen, Sally's husband would leap from his chair and say, "Sal, you look tired. Let's go out for dinner." They happily repeated this routine for many years. This is what makes honesty a complicated issue—the particular circumstances and your motivation should help determine how direct you are.

LEA

In 2005, when the war in Iraq was not going well and antiwar sentiment was intensifying, it became more difficult to find entertainment for White House events. Scheduling entertainers is always tricky because they are often booked years in advance or are touring in another country, so it takes some luck to hit the right combination of "in the country, not booked that night, and willing to work for free." That year we had to add "not unalterably opposed to the Bush administration" to the list of conditions to be met. The situation became more awkward when President Bush would meet entertainers in his travels because they would lie and tell him how much they looked forward to performing at the White House. The president would then mention the conversation to me, I'd call them, and they would be unavailable—every time.

President Bush was far too busy to keep track of celebrities, so it never really mattered, until one night at the senior staff Christmas party when I happened to be seated next to him. He said he'd had a great conversation with a popular country singer, who mentioned he was eager to perform at the White House. I had been on the phone with the singer's manager the week before, and he hadn't just told me no; he'd told me, "*Hell no.*" Without thinking, I replied that I'd just asked his manager and been turned down. I saw a look of disappointment cross the president's face and wished I could take the words back. He always seemed so unfazed by the harshest political attacks that I didn't think he would care about a performer. But as it happened, he was a real fan, and the turndown must have hurt his feelings. I immediately added that I was sure it was just a scheduling conflict. But I realized later that when the president mentioned the musician, I should have agreed that it would be great to have him at the White House and said that I would contact him again. The bad news could have been withheld with no further harm being done, or I could have delivered it more gently.

JEREMY

Being the recipient of brutal honesty has made me think twice about using it myself. In February 2015, just three months before the conclusion of my tenure as social secretary, *Vogue* magazine featured a story about the White House Social Office. I had done my best to keep a low profile as secretary and had participated in virtually no press, so when my coworkers and I were interviewed and photographed, it was exciting and a bit intimidating. We were all worried our wardrobes would not measure up to those of most other people who were profiled in the glamorous magazine, but we were also extremely excited to see the finished product.

Then we found out that a few people in the White House were disgruntled that the Social Office was receiving such attention, feeling that they would have been a better focus for the article. It served no purpose to tell us that. In addition to being painful, it was the first time we had felt any animosity from those individuals, and it changed our positive work dynamic. Such "honesty" turned what should have been a special, exciting experience into something fraught.

To protect our guests and make them feel happy and welcome at all times, we often had to resort to half-truths, and, occasionally, outright lies. We would reframe situations they were complaining about—for example:

> "You don't like your seats for the entertainment? But this spot has the very best acoustics in the room. You're so lucky to be there!"

"I have some exciting news. You're going to be seated with the daughter of the governor at tonight's formal dinner. Won't it be interesting to hear about life in the governor's mansion from the point of view of one of his children? Normally we don't allow children under age fourteen at evenings like this, so this is going to be really special." (We love kids, but if you were invited to a black-tie dinner at the White House, with all the sophistication and glamour that such an evening promises, being seated with a child, however precocious and lovely that child might be, might take something away from the experience.)

"I'm sorry you're disappointed that you aren't seated at the president's table tonight. That's only because the secretary of [Housing and Urban Development, Health and Human Services, Commerce, Transportation] specifically asked that you be at *their* table. We don't get many personal requests like that!"

Sometimes sheltering the truth does more harm than good. Most of us have worked with people who aren't carrying their weight in the workplace, forcing us to make decisions about how we can fix the problem without alienating them. We make these evaluations every day: Should I tell the nice new assistant that he's not getting anyone's phone numbers right when he takes messages? How do I let my coworker know that I'm done covering for her absenteeism and lack of effort on the job?

Do these colleagues need to hear the truth? Yes. But what determines the effectiveness of telling that truth depends on *how* it's told. A new receptionist deserves to be shown what the expectations are for his performance, so telling him that he's very good on the phone and quite fast but needs to write down each telephone number accurately is the way to be honest and optimistic about his work. You owe it to your coworkers to be straight with them before you throw them under the bus by reporting their errors to the boss.

When it comes to your own performance, if you find yourself in a bind at work, remember that it's much easier to answer the question "Why are you telling me this?" than it is to face an angry colleague who says, "Why didn't you tell me this before?" If you have important information that your boss needs to be aware of, such as the fact that a shipment of your top-selling product has been delayed until after Christmas, or you failed to bill a client in a timely fashion and now the monthly balance is off, not telling the truth could snowball, and could even cost you your job. In these situations, sharing the bad news as soon as possible shows integrity and concern for the good of the enterprise.

JEREMY

We always considered the weeks the Obamas were in Martha's Vineyard in August our opportunity to get caught up at work. The first week of September 2011 found me preparing for an East Wing senior staff meeting, the first meeting with Mrs. Obama in more than a month.

Earlier I had received an email from the first lady's chief of staff, Tina Tchen. She suggested that I not mention the upcoming state dinner for Korea, which we had recently learned had been set for October 13. The email caught me off guard. We needed to gather guest lists, have them vetted (which in itself could take six weeks), and get the invitations out in a realistic amount of time. With no chance to speak with Tina before the meeting, I assumed that she didn't want to overwhelm the agenda. Before I could think about it further, I was in front of Mrs. Obama, briefing her on numerous fall events. As I spoke, I contemplated what seemed like a lose/lose situation: Do I ignore FLOTUS's chief of staff or withhold information from Mrs. Obama? And if I kept it from her, how could I assume she wouldn't hear about it from someone else?

So I took a breath and simply said, ". . . and we were just informed of the Korea state dinner date, October 13." Though I could see from her expression that she was surprised, I continued, mentioning the budget and other details. Mrs. Obama expressed her concerns, which mirrored my own, but to my relief, she was otherwise unperturbed.

During the meeting, I didn't dare look in Tina's direction. Afterward, I went to see her and did the only thing I thought might work: I lied. I told her I had not seen the email before the meeting. I could have started off by saying something like, "I'm sorry we didn't get to discuss this earlier . . . ," and explained my reasoning, but at the time, my instinct was to be straight with my boss and then duck and cover with my colleague. It wasn't until years later that I confessed my fib to Tina. We laughed about it, and luckily she forgave me.

THINK ABOUT THE BIGGER PICTURE

It's important to take the long view when considering how honest you want to be with someone. Remember that many working relationships need to continue, even if there's been a conflict, so build for the future.

When you know you've been lied to, consider the best way to manage the situation without provoking a major confrontation.

Challenge a lie, but do it diplomatically. Proceed from the assumption that the person was confused, misled, or given incorrect information. If a coworker lies to your boss and claims that you're to blame for a major product delay, take the coworker aside to calmly address the accusation and insist that you talk to the boss together to clarify the "misunderstanding."

You don't have to call out a coworker directly. Jeremy was in a meeting where Mrs. Obama was telling a staffer that her memo did not have enough details and was critical of her assessment. Jeremy had been at an earlier meeting where he witnessed a coworker directing that colleague to drastically edit her memo. The coworker never said a word in the meeting with the first lady, so afterward, Jeremy informed Mrs. Obama that the employee had in fact done exactly what she was told to do. As a result, she softened her position.

LEA

Not long after I came to the White House, I caught a staffer in an untruth. In my new position, I was thrilled about the idea of showcasing the presidential china and beautiful silver serving pieces, especially the gold vermeil flatware. When I asked one of the ushers about using the flatware for an upcoming dinner, he told me the vermeil set was incomplete and never brought out anymore. I had already caught wind that the use of White House silver and serving pieces was a constant battle; the curators and some ushers, in their roles as preservationists, were quick to deny requests. They didn't even want to show me what was in the collection, and we would regularly find ourselves in excruciatingly polite verbal tussles over access to pieces that had been given to the White House for the sole purpose of being displayed and enjoyed. When I mentioned my disappointment about the vermeil set to another usher, he raised his eyebrows in astonishment: "We have service for sixty in the gold flatware."

From then on, I requested the vermeil flatware whenever it fit the size and formality of an event. It wasn't necessary to have an awkward confrontation with that usher. I knew he was being protective of the collection, and I'm sure he realized I just wanted the parties to be as elegant as possible. We both rose above the moment to ensure we'd work together smoothly in the long run.

JEREMY

I was once talking to someone at an event who began bragging about how close he was to President Obama and the first lady, embellishing it to the point where it was beyond over the top. I knew for a fact that it simply wasn't true, and I was briefly tempted to challenge him, but then I decided it was better to just swallow it. His lies weren't harming anyone's reputation or changing the outcome of anything. They just made his ego feel better. I tried to find a little compassion for him and moved on.

People sometimes say thoughtless things and shouldn't be judged too harshly for them. But if it becomes clear that unhelpful comments are neither unwitting nor singular but represent someone's conscious goading, respond straightforwardly and try to put a stop to it.

Lea's father was a lifelong Democrat, and he seemed to take her different political views as an act of personal disloyalty. For years, he needled her about Republican politicians he didn't like (especially when those politicians were people she worked for). Finally, after one too many occasions of ignoring his cracks or changing the subject, she said, "Dad, we just disagree about politics. Wouldn't it be healthier, since we see each other only a couple of times a year, if we don't talk about this anymore?" Instead of engaging with the specific argument, she made a global one. His political comments all but stopped after that, preserving the warmth of their relationship.

LEA

There is grace and relief in letting some things go. At one of the first parties the Cheneys hosted at the vice president's residence, Marilyn Quayle, former second lady and a former resident of the house, looked around and said loudly, "It used to be so pretty here." Mrs. Cheney and I exchanged amused glances, but she ignored the remark and welcomed Mrs. Quayle warmly. She recognized that Mrs. Quayle was not trying to be insulting; she was simply reminiscing about her time in the residence.

There's a fine, long tradition of lying one's way into a White House party, but few people were as bold as the guest who told Bess Abell, President Johnson's social secretary, that his wife was dying and that it was her last wish to attend a state luncheon for the king and queen of Norway. The invitations for the luncheon had already gone out, and it was at full capacity. Bess went to Lady Bird Johnson and told her about this unusual request, and Mrs. Johnson immediately agreed that Bess should find a way to get this couple into the event, which she did. In the ensuing months, and then years, Bess would run into the man and his perfectly healthy wife around town. Bess had given this guest the benefit of the doubt and been conned, but in the grand scheme of things, inviting them was the right thing to do. Bess warned her successors in the social secretary job about this particular gambit and told us to be deeply skeptical of all "last requests."

CHAPTER 8

The Gift of Loyalty

Friendship is the only cement
that will hold the world together.

WOODROW WILSON

L oyalty flows back and forth like a steady electrical charge at
the White House, strengthening relationships and building
bonds that can last a lifetime. It didn't take long for either of us to
work out whom we could rely on and whom we knew better than
to ask for help—and that's true in any workplace. When loyalty is
strong (and it was mostly *very* strong in the White House), it feels
like there is nothing we can't accomplish together.

Our form of government would never have come into being
without the selfless faith and adherence to the ideals of freedom
and democracy that drove the founders of the nation. Patrick Henry
and George Washington did not have the congenial relationship
that might be expected of two fellow Virginians and revolutionaries.
Henry was violently opposed to the Constitution that Washington
supported. He felt the colonists were simply exchanging a king for a
federal government that could tax with impunity, warning, "Liberty
will be lost and tyranny must and will ensue." Washington called
him an enemy of liberty.

In 1778, when the colonial army was sinking in a series of

137

demoralizing defeats and retreats, Benjamin Rush of Philadelphia, one of the signers of the Declaration of Independence,
formed a cabal to have Washington removed as head of the Continental Army. Rush wrote to Patrick Henry, asking him to join in
the conspiracy. Instead, Henry immediately sent the letter on to
Washington to warn him of the plot. His loyalty to Washington
and their shared goal of independence from England remained
unaffected by their disputes over other matters. Washington
expressed his "most grateful obligations" to Henry, and they continued to be allies until the end of their lives.

Rather than blind obedience, loyalty is a promise of truth and
follow-through. When you work with people who are loyal, you
know they'll perform well because they have a sense of responsibility toward you and toward the enterprise—just as they know
they can count on you for support and guidance in turn.

Teddy Roosevelt's line that "it is better to be faithful than
famous" is a lesson increasingly lost these days, but we've found
that loyalty is a crucial ingredient to achieving success and fulfill-
ment in life. It's an uplifting feeling as well as a teachable social
skill. We've broken down its key elements: practicing discretion,
staying steadfast, and going above and beyond for colleagues,
customers, and friends.

DISCRETION IS AT
THE HEART OF LOYALTY

A loyal person understands how to keep a confidence. Some of
the most devoted people we've known are members of the White
House residence staff. We knew we could trust them because they
never talked about the past occupants of the White House (and

we did ask, out of curiosity and as a kind of informal test). Their unfailing discretion showed their commitment to maintaining the privacy of every president, and it reassured us that they would be equally circumspect about our bosses. We both noticed that even though close proximity to celebrities can be turned into quick cash from the tabloids, very few residence staffers talked to the press, and when they did, their innocuous comments almost always revealed the families in a positive light.

Anyone who works closely around the first family can see how exposed their lives are, so it's natural to feel a sense of protectiveness toward them. Imagine what it's like to know that every word you utter is likely to be repeated by those who hear it, like a game of telephone that ends in a hurtful headline. Imagine that every time you express a frustration or lose your patience (as all of us do), people scurry away to let the rest of the house know you're in a bad mood. The lack of privacy, compounded by the isolation of the White House, would make even the strongest person value loyalty in others. That's why the first families hold the residence staff in such high esteem.

JEREMY

I got a sense of the tact and faithfulness of the residence staff while at Camp David in 2012 for the 38th G-8 Summit. We had been preparing for the leaders for days and had a bit of downtime as we awaited their arrival. As I chatted with the White House butlers, I asked them about some of the previous tenants of the mansion. The stories were all basically positive. The only way I could infer that they liked one more than the others was by how many anecdotes they shared; and by the way they spoke glowingly of George H. W. Bush, it was clear they held him in particularly high esteem. I saw firsthand just how much they revered the family when the senior Bushes came back to the White House in 2013 to celebrate the Points of Light Foundation. As George and Barbara Bush walked into the Diplomatic Reception Room, a group of residence staff was eagerly waiting to greet them. I noticed the tears in the eyes of not only the Bushes but also those who had worked with them more than twenty years before. Such loyalty was inspiring to see.

Take a page from the residence staff, and be circumspect about repeating your friends' and colleagues' personal business. A loyal person doesn't disparage other people behind their backs. Be prepared to politely defend your allies when others speak unkindly of them. Even if the person doing the criticizing doesn't agree with you, he or she will respect your constancy.

Hearing that someone is being critical of you to others can be deeply demoralizing, but try not to take it personally and don't use it as an excuse to start badmouthing that person. This happened several times in Lea's three different jobs in the White House, and though she knew the criticism was more political than pointed (people often try to gain influence for themselves by diminishing others), she always reminded herself that her real loyalty was to the president and first lady and the vice president and second lady.

BEING THERE

The genuine friendship and loyalty between the Obamas and the Bidens was atypical of some of their predecessors. On the morning after the bin Laden announcement, in a quiet moment in the East Room before an event, Jeremy saw the president enter and put his arms around Dr. Biden and Mrs. Obama. It was clear they not only respected each other but had also formed a strong connection built on trust and affection. In the early days of our country, presidents and vice presidents were recent rivals; the vice president was the man who had come in second in the presidential race. Not only that, but the party usually selected the president's running mate, so the chances of their being pals were fairly slim.

This was not the case with Obama and Biden. "I don't like him, I love him," Biden once declared in an interview. When Obama surprised Biden by presenting him with a Presidential Medal of Freedom in an emotional ceremony, he called his veep his "brother." (As a teary-eyed Biden smiled, Obama joked "This gives the Internet one last chance to talk about our bromance.")

Similarly, the devoted partnership between Mrs. Obama and Dr. Biden became more and more evident over time, at Joining Forces events in various parts of the country as well as at functions at the White House. At the funeral of the Bidens' beloved son Beau in June 2015, the president spoke movingly as a member of the family, not a world leader. The love and friendship the two families share is remarkable.

This kind of connection doesn't happen overnight; it's built slowly and carefully through the years. Loyalty means being there—letting others know that you are available and willing to listen or come to their aid. Reach out to a friend who is going through a tough time, either personal or job-related. There are always lots of supporters around when things are going well, but people never forget that you were there when they were most vulnerable.

It's not about empty lip service but specific, repeated gestures of dedication that say, "I'm here for you." If you're at the funeral of a colleague's spouse, saying, "Let me know if I can help," is vague and seems insincere. Instead, think of something particular you can do. Ask if you can bring dinner over Tuesday night, for example, or offer to take the kids to the movies on a Saturday afternoon to give the bereaved a little breathing space.

LEA

Several years ago, my husband was at work in New York when he collapsed with chest pains. He went to the hospital, telling his assistant to let his boss, Stephen Schwarzman, know that he wouldn't be at their meeting later that day. When Schwarzman heard about Wayne, he swung into action. Steve went to the hospital and sat with Wayne for hours while they awaited test results together. He promised to call me the moment there was any word as I flew up to New York to meet them. Happily, Wayne's heart problem was resolved, but our family has never forgotten the extraordinary loyalty and effort Steve displayed for my husband during that frightening ordeal. It was one day in Steve's life, but I've thought gratefully about it many times.

JEREMY

The late Senator Ted Kennedy had a talent for developing deep bonds. After being one of several hosts for a fundraiser for his Senate reelection, I received a handwritten note from him—but also phone calls on Easter, July Fourth, and other holidays. He would call just to chat, as if we were old friends. My parents had always thought so highly of him, and now I saw why.

Bill Carrick, Senator Kennedy's political director for years, told me how he learned from the start that his boss stressed the importance of personal relationships with his colleagues. When Senator John Stennis of Mississippi went into the hospital one weekend, and Kennedy was not told until he got back from the Cape the following Monday, he called Carrick and said, "Bill, I need your help on politics, I need your strategic help, but most of all I need you to tell me when colleagues go into the hospital!"

This is what it takes to establish yourself as a person who can be counted on:

Keep your word. As always, consistency is key. Doing what you say you're going to do shows that you're dependable and inspires fealty. It's much more rewarding (not to mention less lonely) to go through life with friends you can rely on rather than going it alone.

Give your honest take when asked. If you have tough news to share with a friend, make sure you are also communicating your support. Jeremy had a friend who was really hoping for a key appointment. It became clear that it was not going to happen, yet no one wanted to be the one to tell her. Jeremy met with her and told her what she should expect. She was disappointed but appreciated his being forthright with her.

Be unconditional in your support. Once you've established that you're fully supportive of someone, don't hang back. Be unstinting in your efforts to help that person succeed. You can't be a little bit loyal, in the same way that you can't be a little bit pregnant. Friends and colleagues alike will appreciate your commitment and enthusiasm.

JEREMY

All of us have our ups and downs in life, and we remember most fondly those who back us up no matter what we're going through. Vicki Kennedy, the wife of the late Senator Ted Kennedy, is gifted at making others feel valued. We had met numerous times over the years and always had enjoyable conversations. I received notes from her at various times during my tenure, but most touching were the emails she sent after I left my White House position, when she asked how I was doing and what I was working on next, and sending her best wishes. It meant a lot.

LEA

When I first came to Washington, I worked with an elderly Dutch woman at the Center for Strategic and International Studies at Georgetown University. Ilse Muller grew up in Indonesia, where her father worked for Royal Dutch Shell, and she was trapped there when the Japanese occupied the country at the beginning of World War II. She spent her teenage years in a Japanese women's internment camp, living under unspeakably harsh conditions, and the experience left her with a unique appreciation for life and a stout supportiveness of the people she cared about.

She took a kindly interest in me, and we often went to lunch at a nearby Indonesian restaurant where she would order for us in perfect Malay, introducing my midwestern palate to exotic dishes like *nasi goreng* and sweet *martabak*. She took time with me, pressing me to slow down and be more accurate in my work, encouraging my plans for graduate school, and gently pushing me to have fun and be less serious about everything. The effect of having one person in my life who always offered sound guidance gave me such a lift.

Her friendship became especially important when I got engaged. My parents were opposed to the marriage, refusing to pay for the wedding and initially declining to attend. (Wayne was the first Jewish person my mother had ever met, and my parents did not approve.) What should have been one of the happiest times in my life became a daily headwind of opposition from two people whose approval I'd always sought. Ilse was my rock through all of it, and it was such a blessing to have a mature, loyal friend who was happy about the wedding and smiling through the entire ceremony. My parents came to love Wayne over time, but I'll never forget how important Ilse's unswerving fidelity was in those early, emotional days.

LOYALTY FLOWS
IN BOTH DIRECTIONS

Loyalty isn't only important between peers and colleagues. As business leaders know, it's also vital to a successful enterprise. Today companies have to do more than pay a person to expect steadfastness in return. This means giving employees a chance to have input into how their professional goals can best be met, creating opportunity for career growth, building cooperation throughout all parts of an organization, and showing employees that you care about their individual and collective well-being. If you're in a leadership position, show appreciation. Stand up for your staff members. Give people the motivation they need to do their best for you.

Keeping an open-door policy also engenders loyalty. In many ways, an office environment is like a family; we bond with the people we can talk to easily. Giving praise, communicating regularly with staff, and providing opportunities for further learning and training help employees feel they're growing in their jobs and builds a sense of dedication to the company.

Lea always knew that if a delicate problem arose and she needed advice, she could pick up the phone and have a frank conversation with Joshua Bolten, the White House chief of staff. In fact, he had reached out to her when he began in his job and urged her to call him anytime. His openness made the interaction between the Social Office and the West Wing much smoother than it had been in the past, and his collegiality extended throughout the White House and made the whole atmosphere more productive and congenial.

Giving employees a sense of purpose and making them feel they're part of something larger than themselves is a wonderful way to kindle loyalty. It's human nature to seek to please those we like, and that expression of loyalty will be returned and amplified many times over.

JEREMY

When you're working hard for an organization or a cause and something challenging happens, knowing that those higher up have your back can be a tremendous relief. One prominent Democratic donor who hoped to host an event for Senator Obama began by asking for an enormous amount of one-on-one time and commitments on a wide range of issues. She grew irate when asked to temper her expectations and started screaming at anyone from the campaign staff who would listen to her. I was the one she spoke to with the most colorful language.

After our one-sided "conversation," I called Penny Pritzker, the national finance chair, to relay the experience. I held my breath for Penny's response; this was, after all, a longtime major donor to the party. Penny told me not to worry: this person would not be hosting any events. Penny, who would become Obama's secretary of commerce, showed us that her true loyalty was to those devoting their lives to the campaign.

LEA

One late afternoon, I had a visit from Laura Bush, who had a habit of popping into different East Wing offices and asking in a friendly way, "What are you working on?" (These visits in themselves were real morale boosters.) I was searching for menu ideas for the Senate Spouses' Luncheon and had come upon a photo and recipe of a beautiful dish with edible flowers sealed within very thin layers of pappardelle pasta on a bed of microgreens with a light lemon sauce (we social secretaries never forget the food details). She looked at the photo in the book and said, "May I borrow this?" and then got up and left. Her personal aide returned it a few days later. That day, Joan Doty, who worked in the first lady's Correspondence Office, said, "Mrs. Bush brought in a book the other day and showed us a picture of a meal you're planning for the Senate spouses. She said, 'This is why Lea Berman is so good at her job.'" I blushed at the unexpected compliment, and my feelings of loyalty for Laura Bush deepened even further in that moment.

CUSTOMER LOYALTY

Loyalty has real value whether you're on the giving or the receiving end. That's why loyalty is so appealing: the mutual benefit draws us together and makes us feel good. But it's not only about a sense of personal well-being; loyalty drives organizations of all sizes. As any businessperson will tell you, a small percentage of repeat customers typically accounts for an outsize amount of sales. When you go to the same coffee shop every day because the coffee is good, the servers remember your name, and every tenth cup is free, everybody wins.

Whether it's for a customer or a client or a White House guest, creating a sense of loyalty is, at its heart, about making people feel remembered, valued, and heard. No matter what your line of work, when you make an effort to instill loyalty, you're sending a message that you're interested in going beyond a business transaction in order to build a relationship.

LEA

Morgan's is a small pharmacy in Georgetown that has been delivering prescriptions to Washingtonians for over a hundred years. I once had a badly infected hand after being bitten by a dog, and my doctor called in a prescription to Morgan's for antibiotics late on a Friday afternoon, not realizing that the pharmacy was closed and would not be open again until Monday. Barry, the pharmacist, picked up the message on the after-hours voice mail, called my husband directly, and arranged to meet him at the (closed) pharmacy to fill the prescription for me that night. That's the kind of service that builds staunch customer loyalty—and what a rare and deeply appreciated thing it is.

JEREMY

My father, who was an attorney in San Antonio, had a very diverse client list; he worked with community organizers, teachers, politicians, and business leaders. One summer afternoon when I was a teenager, visiting my dad's office for the day, Angelo Drossos, the owner of the San Antonio Spurs at that time, said to me as he was leaving, "You know, a lot of people ask me why I still go to your dad. Our politics are so different, and he's not at some big corporate law firm. But when I only had a small food cart and not a dime to my name, your dad was there for me. He was there when I had nothing. I will always remember that."

Years later, when my father passed, another friend, Bill Harden, wrote a letter that appeared in the paper, which said in part: "My best friend died this morning. . . . He had a wonderful sense of humor, and his laugh may be what I miss most. . . . If you didn't know him personally, I wish you had, but I want you to know that he worked his whole life on your behalf. . . . I have known many people during my life but have never known a better human. By the way, I am a life-long conservative Republican." My father would probably have been embarrassed that the letter was in the paper, but I was proud and very touched by their loyal bond.

The Obamas also knew how to demonstrate loyalty. When they went from fundraising in the spring of 2007 for Barack Obama's unlikely bid to be president to moving into the White House, they took many of the people who had been there with them from the start. I'll never forget an early encounter I had with Mrs. Obama in Los Angeles, where we had just finished a fundraiser. She was heading on to San Diego and was driving a rental minivan; she had her two girls with her, and one aide, Melissa Winter. Bottled water sat in the cup holder; there was nothing about the car that implied "future VIP." I told her that a group of us from the California finance office would try to get there in advance. Her response, a portent of her future role as Mom in Chief, was to ask us to just make sure we drove safely.

Less than twenty months later, Michelle Obama was first lady. Melissa Winter would become her deputy chief of staff and continue with her after the White House. I would become social secretary, and others who were there in the early days also went on to key positions in the administration. Longtime relationships were important to the Obamas, although of course we still had to prove ourselves every day.

STAND BY YOUR PERSON OR CAUSE

Presidents are judged by their displays of public loyalty. Dwight Eisenhower did not come to the defense of his mentor, General George C. Marshall, when Marshall came under attack by Senator Joseph McCarthy during the 1952 presidential campaign. Eisenhower considered McCarthy to be utterly reprehensible and was prepared to defend Marshall in an important campaign speech, but the political realities of McCarthy's popular appeal at the time overcame his best intentions and he left the part of his speech about George Marshall out at the last minute. This surprised and disappointed some of Eisenhower's supporters and is said to have troubled him for the rest of his life.

George H. W. Bush stood by his vice president, Dan Quayle, when advisors urged him to dump him from the ticket in 1992 because they thought he was a liability. His supporters may not have liked his choice, but they grudgingly admitted that Bush exhibited characteristic loyalty in sticking with Quayle.

Loyalty requires vigilance and courage. Abraham Lincoln said, "Be with a leader when he is right, stay with him when he is still right, but leave him when he is wrong." Sadly, this happens less frequently in politics today. When our personal values are not in sync with the values of our bosses and leaders, it's essential that we end the association, or risk losing touch with who we really are.

CHAPTER 9

Own Your Mistakes

✧ ✧ ✧

The time is always right to do the right thing.
MARTIN LUTHER KING JR.

In 1987, President Reagan made an unusual statement regarding the Iran-Contra affair in an Oval Office speech to the American people. The Reagan administration, while negotiating the release of American hostages in Iran, had secretly sold arms to that country at a time when such sales were under embargo, with the intention of using the proceeds to arm the Nicaraguan Contra rebels. Taking responsibility for his administration's participation in an international fiasco, Reagan frankly admitted he had made a mistake.

This was a remarkable moment, given that presidents are not known for fulsome and frequent apologies—at least until the memoirs are written. But Ronald Reagan's attitude puts him in good company with many of our most creative innovators. "Embrace every failure," Steve Jobs famously said. "Own it, learn from it, and take full responsibility for making sure that next time, things will turn out differently."

So why *do* we try so hard to avoid mistakes? We fear them and stay awake at night thinking about how *not* to make them. We start going down the path of worst-case scenarios: too many failed tests in school and you get bad grades, too many bad grades and you don't get into college, too many mistakes at work and your professional options shrink. Thinking that way is unproductive, but we understand that sometimes it's hard to stop.

Let's put aside these imaginary failures for a moment. What happens when you've actually made a misstep? We realize that there are few things more difficult than acknowledging an error; it's so much easier to blame others or to hope that a mistake is small enough to go unnoticed. Expressing genuine remorse, however, is essential when you need to right a wrong at work or put an injured friendship back on healthy footing. Having the awareness to recognize when you've blundered and the boldness to do something about it requires exercising many of the elements of emotional intelligence that we've discussed: confidence, courage, empathy, and a willingness to make yourself vulnerable. It doesn't feel good to be in the wrong, but it feels even worse to do nothing, allowing others to believe we don't know or care enough to make it up to them.

Owning your mistakes rests on four key concepts: give yourself room to fail, apologize sincerely and soon, make amends, and let it go. Try to think of a mistake as an opportunity to prove yourself.

GIVE YOURSELF ROOM TO FAIL

Mistakes are inevitable, yet many of our choices in daily life are narrowed by fears of failure. Do you hesitate to introduce yourself to an important person at a party because she might find you too self-promoting? Do you refrain from suggesting a potential solution to a problem at work because you don't want to be wrong?

We become so focused on the bad thing that might happen that we limit potential good outcomes—and ourselves.

The job of social secretary is one of high stakes and high visibility, and we often found ourselves focused on avoiding the negative (*Try not to mess this up!*) rather than seeking out the positive (*This event is going to be fantastic!*). Over time, we concluded that this self-imposed negativism created a distraction from our ability to do our jobs successfully.

When you live in dread of disappointment, you instantly curtail your ability to maneuver around it. Instead, remind yourself of what the worst possible outcome could be. If it's outlandish, dismiss it. If it really could happen, focus on the concrete steps you can take to ensure it doesn't. Break things down into manageable parts, and don't be afraid to ask others for help. You may feel uncomfortable about involving others, but it's usually less embarrassing than failing spectacularly all by yourself.

JEREMY

When I left my government affairs job after nine years to start a political fundraising and consulting business, I was filled with trepidation. What if I was making a giant mistake and the business tanked? It didn't help that a lot of my friends asked: "Why would you leave such a good position?" Even my mother questioned my decision. But I knew it was time to make a change and that waiting would make leaving even more challenging (the idea of "perfect timing" is usually a fiction). I had to redirect my fear of failure into a more constructive frame of mind, telling myself that even though I was entering a completely different landscape, I was ready to do so and would be opening up exciting new possibilities. Luckily, despite some bumps in the road, the business was eventually a success. One of the first clients was Obama for President in early 2007, which of course led to opportunities beyond my imagination.

LEA

The need to make everything right and put all things in order is difficult to overcome, but it's my established MO. I hadn't been at the White House very long before I began to see that this approach was a liability.

Once, Mrs. Bush asked me to invite all of the people who'd been in her and her husband's wedding party for a private anniversary celebration at the residence. I received a list of names from her personal aide and began calling guests. Most of the couples were from Texas, and I wanted to give them as much time as possible to make their travel arrangements. I used the Friends and Family database to find a phone number for one couple on the list—I'll call them "Mr. and Mrs. Jones." I talked to Mr. Jones, and he said they would be delighted to come. When I sent the list of responses upstairs to the aide, she called me back and said, "You invited the wrong Jones! You were supposed to invite the brother—*he* was the one who was in the wedding party. One is Chris and the other is Nick."

I called back Chris Jones and gently explained my mistake. Mr. Jones said he completely understood—but that he and his wife had been invited to the White House, and they were coming.

Now I'd turned my slipup into a mess. Of course the man was right: an invitation to the White House is not something to be proffered and then plucked away. I went upstairs to tell Mrs. Bush what had happened and to apologize. I told her I wanted to let her know about it as soon as possible. She gave me an amused look and then shrugged her shoulders. "Just invite them both," she said, as if she was surprised that I hadn't worked that out for myself. I felt foolish—but at the same time I was beginning to understand that my outsize fear of making mistakes was out of sync with the reality of the consequences.

APOLOGIZE SINCERELY AND SOON

When you've misspoken or misstepped, acknowledge it right away. The longer a gaffe remains unexposed, the more serious it can become, and the longer someone has to wait for an apology, the less likely he'll be to accept it. Express regret as soon you realize your blunder, and be specific in acknowledging what you've done. If you can't decide whether an error is worth bringing up, remember that saying you're sorry right away is almost always better than not saying it (though don't overdo it; apologizing constantly about everything under the sun dilutes the impact).

A sincere apology can be as therapeutic for the person making it as it is for the person receiving it. But don't press for forgiveness. It's rare for a person to forgive a transgression immediately. It might even be necessary, after some time passes, to express your regret again, to clear the air and prevent resentment from growing.

JEREMY

One evening in October 2011, my friend Tammy Haddad, founder of her own media consultant firm, invited me to a small gathering at the Jefferson Hotel. I was having dinner in George-town with friends, and Tammy told me to bring them along. We walked into the elegant private "tea room" to find a handful of other guests, including former prime minister Gordon Brown and his wife, Sarah. Luckily, the newspapers didn't catch the exchange between my friend Bill Huggins and Gordon Brown. Brown was joking about some political situation when Bill said, "You know how to tell when a politician is lying?" Before Bill got to the punch line, Brown interrupted and said: "When their lips move." Brown then asked if Bill needed another drink and walked away.

I looked at Bill with surprise. "I can't believe you just tried to tell that joke," I said. Bill was puzzled until I told him he had been speaking to the former prime minister of England, who had left office the previous year. Bill had had no idea. When Brown returned with drinks, Bill immediately apologized. Brown laughed it all off, patting Bill on the back. It was a class act on the part of the prime minister.

LEA

I also saw how important it is to step lively after a blunder. Many years ago, Wayne and I were guests on the PepsiCo corporate jet. It was one of my first experiences flying on a private plane, and I was very excited. When the flight attendant asked what I wanted to drink, I asked for a Coke. The attendant blanched and said, "We only carry Pepsi products, ma'am." I looked at him and said sheepishly, "Then I'll have a water." He nodded and walked away. I felt embarrassed by the doubly rude and thoughtless thing I'd done. Instead of cowering in my seat, though, I went back to the galley and apologized to the attendant, who seemed to find it very amusing. No harm done on that occasion, but it was a great reminder to think before speaking.

After having had plenty of practice, we've learned some things about how to say sorry succinctly and sincerely.

Don't equivocate. A successful apology requires contrition, and also a bit more. As Ben Franklin said, "Never ruin an apology with an excuse." Express regret in an unqualified way, without trying to justify your behavior.

Take your time. Body language and setting are important. Find a quiet place where you won't be disturbed. Don't rush through your apology; you'll seem uncomfortable or, worse, disingenuous. Look the person in the eye, relax your face, let your hands be at rest, and don't cross your arms defensively.

The words you use matter. Starting with, "I wish it hadn't happened," is not an apology. Your efforts will likewise sink if you say, "Listen, I'm sorry if you . . ." It doesn't matter what the rest of the sentence is. The *if* places the responsibility on the person you're apologizing to rather than on you, where it belongs.

MAKE AMENDS

Sometimes being contrite isn't enough. If you've bungled something, first step up and accept responsibility; then move in as soon as possible to remedy the problem. As we learned firsthand, most workplace snafus can be corrected as long as you're fast on your feet. If the graphics for a major presentation aren't done because you underestimated how long it would take to put them together, be the first to say you'll work all weekend getting it right.

LEA

President Bush often invited world leaders to his ranch in Crawford, Texas. In fact, a diplomat once told me that an invitation to Crawford was more coveted than an invitation to the White House because it implied a personal relationship with the president. My job was to work out the menus for these visits, arrange for the flowers and table linens, and have the pastry chef make the signature cookies: an American flag entwined with the flag of the visiting leader's country.

The elaborately decorated cookies were a White House specialty and had become somewhat legendary. When Israeli Prime Minister Ariel Sharon was scheduled to be at the ranch the following day, I received a panicked call from the White House pastry chef: the cookies were still on his kitchen counter, but the president had already left. I started calling around in the hope that someone was still headed to Texas. Eventually I learned of a support plane leaving that evening. An usher delivered the cookies to the plane, and I made sure someone was waiting for them at the Crawford end. It didn't matter whose mistake it had been. The error was corrected, and that was what mattered.

Quick thinking was similarly required when Laurie Firestone, social secretary to President George H. W. Bush and Barbara Bush, looked at the dessert platters that were about to go into the dining room at a state dinner in honor of President Carlos Salinas de Gortari of Mexico. She was horrified to see that the platters featured little marzipan houses with candy versions of a sleeping Mexican worker leaning against the house. She couldn't believe her eyes: it was the worst imaginable stereotype and just the sort of image President Salinas de Gortari had been working hard to erase. Laurie stepped in front of the butlers holding the platters, plucked off the sleeping figures, and replaced each with a flower, thereby avoiding a confectionery crisis.

JEREMY

Shortly after I started at the White House, I was invited to a black-tie dinner, and I asked a friend to join me as my date. At the table, we were seated next to each other. I didn't think about it at the time, but during the dinner, the hostess walked over and mentioned that the place cards had been moved and that I was in the wrong seat. I apologized and asked if there was anything I could do, but she demurred. I looked at my friend, he shrugged his shoulders, and the evening continued without further comment— or so I thought.

Over the next weeks I heard from various people, including a few of my social secretary predecessors, that I had upset the hostess; she believed I had made the change. I told my friend about the fallout, and he admitted that he had changed the cards, not thinking it was a big deal. So I reached out to the hostess, invited her to lunch, and apologized for poor judgment on my part. I told her I hoped we could move forward. I did not mention that my friend was the culprit. That was less important than to simply express remorse and promise it wouldn't happen again. I became a regular guest at her home, and the two of us remained friends throughout my years at the White House.

· · ·

Here are a few basic tips about fixing mistakes:

Don't blame others. This wastes valuable time and energy and does not make you look like a team player. Accept your role in what happened.

Find a way to make it right. Write down a list of solutions, choose your course, and jump into action.

Ask for help. Many people are too proud or consider it a sign of weakness, but soliciting and accepting help is a sign of strength and a great way to build a sense of trust and shared purpose.

Pitch in. When you find a mistake, take every opportunity to fix it, even if it's not yours. Think of it as taking one for the team. People will notice and be grateful for the support.

LEA

I made a potentially monumental mistake in my early days at the White House. Fortunately, when I admitted it and asked my coworkers to bail me out, they banded together to make it work.

It all started with what I thought was a brilliant idea: we would kill two birds with one stone by combining the annual Congressional Picnic with an *In Performance at the White House* Public Broadcasting System television special. Through my ignorance, I created a scenario that nearly sank both events. The picnic is one of the largest happenings of the year at the White House, with more than twelve hundred guests on the South Lawn. This particular year, it featured a carousel, tables groaning with barbecue, eight kinds of pie, and an ice cream bar.

In Performance at the White House is a long-running series that

allows viewers to share special evenings of top-grade entertainment featured at the White House. We needed talent for the
summer picnic and were already working on a show featuring
Broadway performers with an Americana theme with PBS, so it
seemed logical to organize the show to be the entertainment for
the picnic.

I'd never experienced a Congressional Picnic before and didn't
understand that it took our full resources to pull it off each year.
The chefs prepared for days, the grounds crew needed a week to
set up the food tents and a hundred picnic tables, and the Secret
Service had to check into the backgrounds of everyone from the
carousel operator to the tent crews. As soon as I got into the
details, I realized with horror that making these two events happen at the same time was setting us up to fail on both fronts.

I went to chief usher Gary Walters and threw myself at his
mercy, admitting that I'd made a terrible mistake and that we
were now committed to both Congress and PBS. I asked him to
help me make it work, knowing I was placing unfair demands
on him and the staff—which I vowed to never do again. He was
gracious and understanding and made it clear to the staff that
this was a never-to-be-repeated circumstance. We hired dozens
of extra staff from a local caterer and farmed out some of the food
prep. Grounds crews worked nearly around the clock to have both
event areas ready—and everything went smoothly, to my great
relief.

As I headed home after the picnic late that night, the Pointer
Sisters' song "Jump!" came on the radio, reminding me of the
scene in *Love Actually* when Hugh Grant (as the British prime
minister) dances by himself, celebrating his first big success in his
job. I rolled the windows down and sang along at the top of my
lungs, never having felt so relieved and grateful in my entire life.

My colleagues at the White House saved my bacon that week. Because I admitted my error as soon as I realized it, took responsibility, and asked for help, we were able to pull together to fix what could have been a disastrous night. The truth is that people are usually willing to pitch in if we aren't too proud to ask.

LET IT GO

Forgiveness is liberating. When you can find compassion for a person who has wronged you, you release the power that person has over you. It's possible to forgive a person without excusing what he or she did. Holding a grudge exacerbates the wrong you've already suffered by making you revisit it again and again. How much better to let go of the sense of injustice and bitterness instead of having it haunt you for years.

Leaders don't fear their mistakes, but are open to correction and to learning from their failures. They also ask for forgiveness—and give it generously. This goes for you too. Don't dwell on your own mistakes. Allow yourself a little grace period and then remind yourself that you were doing your best, stop feeling guilty, and move on. Obsessing over a problem just keeps it alive.

LEA

Washington is not an easy place for a stay-at-home mom, as I was in my thirties. In a city full of ambitious hyperachievers, the idea that a woman has made a conscious choice to make motherhood her primary occupation is not fully respected in many circles. I came to dread going to cocktail parties, where the first (and inevitable) question was, "What do you do?" (For the record, it is impolite to begin any conversation with that question. It's like stating that you're assessing the possible value of the encounter based on the relative importance of the person you've just met.) On one occasion, when I told a woman who asked me that question that I was at home with my children, she turned on her heel and walked away without further comment. Most were less obvious in their disinterest, but the message was clear and my confidence shaken.

As I grew more comfortable with my life choices, I stopped caring about what people thought and forgave them their trespasses. People rarely apologize for an offensive comment or slight, because they usually don't realize they're being hurtful. It's easiest to give them the benefit of the doubt. It's all so insignificant in the overall pattern of life. What a great gift it is to finally understand that.

JEREMY

For years, I beat myself up for not finishing college. I now realize that I was struggling with my sexuality and fearful to reveal that I was hurting. What I should have done was ask for help, but instead I suffered in silence and eventually dropped out of school. I look back and see that if I had asked for help, I likely would have been able to finish my studies, but it took me many years to consider what I had learned from the experience. Now when I start to get overwhelmed or stressed out, I know that asking for help is the smart, effective, and responsible thing to do. In time, I found my way. It's reasonable to have regrets—but it's important to forgive yourself too.

Remember that no matter how carefully we try to avoid mistakes, unforeseen circumstances will occur. If nothing else, you might be left with a great story.

When the carefully planned visit to California by the queen of England on her royal yacht was disrupted by heavy rains and mudslides in 1983, a much-anticipated excursion to President Reagan's Southern California ranch became a lot more complicated. The royal yacht was forced by weather conditions to dock in San Francisco, and State Department protocol officer (and later White House social secretary) Gahl Hodges Burt flew into high gear, organizing within a few hours an impromptu dinner for the queen at Trader Vic's, the city's venerable and beloved Polynesian restaurant.

When the queen and her consort, Prince Philip, arrived at Trader Vic's, Gahl made polite small talk with them, asking if they had a favorite restaurant in London. Prince Philip replied that they hadn't been to a restaurant since their son Charles's christening some forty years before. Gahl had the uncomfortable recognition that their choice of dinner locations might not have been the best one. To make matters worse, at the end of the meal, fortune cookies were passed around and the dinner guests took turns reading their fortunes aloud. Muffie Brandon, the White House social secretary at the time, remembers that the queen read hers and then turned to her husband and said, "Philip, what did you get?" He opened it, hesitated, then read aloud: "You will marry a very wealthy person." Silence ensued. It was not the evening that Gahl and Muffie might have wished for, but thankfully they got through the rest of the evening without further incident.

This was not the first time the queen had witnessed a gaffe on these shores. During an earlier visit to celebrate the American Bicentennial, President Ford invited the queen to have the first dance at the state dinner in her honor. To the surprise of social secretary Maria Downs, the Marine Band began to play "The Lady Is a Tramp" as the president escorted the queen to the dance floor. Some time later, Maria asked the president if he had real-ized what the band was playing while he danced with the queen.

"Oh, yes," he said.

And did he think that the queen also knew?

"Oh," he said. "Yes."

Mistakes make us human. The more comfortable you are with them, the more you show you're a person of humor, flexibility, and character.

CHAPTER 10

Keep Smiling,
and Other Ways to Deal
with Difficult People

No one can make you feel inferior without your consent.

ELEANOR ROOSEVELT

W e very much hope you can skip this chapter because you don't have any problem people in your life. We like to assume most people are like us—hoping to get through the day as agreeably as possible. Truly incorrigible people are actually pretty rare, but they seem larger than life because their bad behavior has such an outsize effect. One challenging individual can change the atmosphere of a room simply by walking into it, dampening moods and sowing dread. But difficult people *can* be managed, with perspective, deflection, and patience—and by remembering your own self-worth.

Dealing with intractable types requires a certain delicacy; we tend to move gingerly around them, as if we're afraid to awaken a sleeping giant. That fear is exactly what an insecure, aggressive person relies on in order to hold power over us. We've used examples from our own lives and careers to illustrate points throughout this book, but it wouldn't be in the spirit of treating people well if we skewered the difficult people we've known by naming them publicly. It's tempting (and certainly in the tradition of score-settling books about D.C.), but if there's one thing we'd like everyone to take away from our book, it's that rising above petty, rude, or intimidating behavior shows strength and integrity. The details of some stories in this chapter may have been changed to protect the guilty, but there are still plenty of suggestions for handling any antagonist or bully whose behavior is upsetting or unproductive.

There's an ailment found among some White House staff known as "White House–itis." Symptoms include delusional views of your own power, disdain for those who work beneath you, and relentless self-promotion. This could probably describe the traits of many people who are disagreeable to work with. These well-known types—the backstabbers, egomaniacs, envy mongers, and gossips—don't have to have a reason to make the lives of others difficult; they just love the drama of confrontation and enjoy making everyone around them feel small so that they can feel superior.

In the working world, researchers are beginning to discover the price that companies pay for a jerk in their midst. A study of public service workers found what many of us could confirm through experience that "people leave managers, not companies." When you consider that 46 percent of new hires don't last eighteen months and 89 percent of those who leave do so because they don't like the culture of the office, it becomes clear how costly a bad boss or truculent colleague can be in terms of both economics and morale.

The first on your list of people who deserves to be treated well is you. We've sorted out five different strategies to help you deal with tricky types: ignore, stay good-humored, deflect and manage, emotionally disengage, and speak up when the situation demands it.

IGNORE, IGNORE, IGNORE

We all know people who like to stir the pot. It's the coworker making mean-spirited cracks about another staffer who is out of the room or telling an off-color joke to get a rise out of you. Since these types thrive on attention, the strongest remedy is to look the other way. It stifles that negative energy like a wet blanket.

When someone behaves badly in a public setting, like the person who keeps asking for ice cream samples as a line builds impatiently behind him, or the driver who revs into the parking space someone else was clearly waiting for, the best recourse is to refuse to be drawn into it. Think of such conduct as you would a bad cold: something that can infect you in an instant and drag you down. Whenever possible, preserve your sanity by tuning the troublemaker out as if he were a staticky radio station.

At one White House Easter Egg Roll, Laura Bush's press secretary was in the middle of a live *Today Show* interview, talking about what guests could expect on the South Lawn that morning. Just then, a costumed Curious George came up behind her and started making unmistakably lewd gestures. The cameraman cut to a close-up, and soon after, the teenager in the monkey suit was escorted off the grounds. Realizing the incident was outrageous but harmless, the press secretary remained unfazed on-screen and continued the interview. Afterward, she looked as if she could have used a stiff drink, but she shook it off and went on to do her other interviews. Brava!

FIND THE LAUGH

Try to locate the humor in these moments, even if it's dark. When a particularly demanding diva was asked to sing at the White House, we would be unfailingly polite while she threw tantrums, canceled the gig, asked for the impossible, and then showed up at the last minute to perform. Jokes about all the places we'd like to tell her to go were passed around among the White House staff who dealt with her, gently and in a spirit of camaraderie, because we all knew it would be over in a few hours. It gave us an esprit de corps and put the behavior in perspective. We didn't feel burdened; we were amused.

LEA

"The swamp," as Washington has been called, is a small place, and it's not always possible to avoid prickly personalities. I've learned to lean into insulting comments with such good humor that the person realizes there's really no point in continuing, or to respond so blandly that the bad-mouther has nowhere left to go. One woman I know always makes a point of telling me, "I never see you *anywhere!*" Washington translation: you must not be getting the good party invitations anymore. I always say the same thing in reply, "I never see you anywhere either, and it's such a disappointment!" Be vague, be lighthearted—but never let yourself be hurt.

STEER THE CONVERSATION

Every once in a while, we are faced with someone whose bad behavior we can't ignore. All White House social offices, in all administrations, are adept at deflecting and managing demanding and difficult people, especially when working with celebrities, which is a big part of our job. Many entertainers who come to perform at the White House don't understand that it's not a theater venue; the White House is best suited to unplugged performances—an entertainer, a spotlight, an instrument. There are only two state rooms that can accommodate a stage, no rehearsal spaces, and the food that's available is what can be made in the White House kitchens (allowing for the fact that the chefs are probably in the midst of preparing a four-course meal for hundreds of people).

Whenever we received a long list of a performer's requirements—"Must have gold star on dressing room door" (what dressing room?) or recipes for six vegan, gluten-free meals the celebrity would be willing to eat—we did a lot of rolling with it (and, we must admit, some behind-the-scenes eye rolling). Then we smiled and did what we could to be accommodating. Sometimes we would take performers on a tour of the parts of the White House most people never see, showing them the burn marks on the stone foundation from when the British set fire to the White House in 1812, or Richard Nixon's bowling alley in the basement. The most popular distractions were invariably the First Pets. Every time we took miffed VIPs to the South Lawn to romp with the dogs, they always seemed to forget whatever it was they were unhappy about.

There are difficult people who sail in and out of our lives, and there are those with whom we are forced to deal every day. If you're stuck with an unreasonably taxing boss, try to understand what drives him or her and strive to minimize your vulnerabilities. If your boss tends to blame others for his mistakes, use email to get his decisions in writing and confirm verbal instructions with a follow-up email—time-consuming, yes, but an act of self-preservation. If she's a micromanager, anticipate what she's likely to want and do it before she asks. If he's hot-tempered, keep track of his work pressures as they ebb and flow so you don't attempt a sensitive conversation at an inopportune time. Don't let anyone's bad temper and unprofessionalism affect your own work performance: be the person you wish your boss would be in your dealings with others.

LEA

I once worked for a boss whose aggression and micromanaging drained the energy and enthusiasm of everyone who worked for him. A Jekyll-and-Hyde personality who pretended to be a warm and benevolent manager in the presence of *his* boss, he turned into a snarling egomaniac with a hair-trigger temper when the boss left the room. Turnover was incredibly high; he went through a personal assistant every six months, and we watched in sadness as these young people left, hollow-eyed and emotionally beaten down.

Worst of all, there was no mechanism for us to communicate to his higher-ups; an air of quiet despair hung over the office. Because I had committed to stay for a set period of time, my only recourse was to find ways to work around him. He constantly shot down my ideas for events, so I began every pitch by saying that this particular occasion would require his presence, knowing how much he loved the limelight. Of course, he didn't want to get involved with the details (to my relief); he just showed up and took credit. All that mattered to me was that events were taking place, and once I discovered how well this tactic worked, I used it repeatedly.

Sometimes you can manage a difficult colleague by quietly appealing to a higher authority for help. Lucy Breathitt, the diminutive and energetic White House social secretary for the six years of the Nixon administration, found herself in the unenviable position of dealing with a man who would become notorious for his brash behavior, Nixon's chief of staff, H. R. Haldeman. Haldeman gradually shut out Nixon's long-serving and trusted former aides, gaining power and influence by reorganizing the White House staff structure to better funnel control through his office, a configuration that basically remains in place today. (Neither Presidents Kennedy nor Johnson had chiefs of staff; their White Houses were organized more like a wheel, with the president in the hub and his aides as spokes in the wheel who reported directly to him. Haldeman required other aides to go through him to get to the president.)

Haldeman began interfering with scheduled events. He independently decided that state dinners could take place outside Washington and scheduled a dinner for the president of Mexico in San Diego, over the objections of Lucy, who understood all too well how problematic such an occasion would be. Haldeman retorted that Lucy would not be needed in San Diego—until the plans began to unravel and he was forced to call her in at the last minute to save the evening. At her wit's end, Lucy went to Mrs. Nixon to ask for her help with Haldeman. The first lady confronted both Haldeman and Nixon together to demand that they stay out of event planning at the White House, and Haldeman interfered less after that (though he never really stopped).

Another effective strategy is to impose rules that narrow the ways a fractious colleague can behave badly. Being able to fall back on a workplace policy gives the difficult person less room in which to operate.

If a coworker is acting obstructively and you are unable to deflect and manage his behavior, you might have to have a hard conversation. Granted, it takes courage to confront coworkers and tell them that they're not helping the cause. But in the end, this straightforward approach is one of the most direct routes to a resolution. Be kind, direct, and prepared with unemotional statements. As former senator Daniel Patrick Moynihan once said, "We are all entitled to our own opinions, but we are not entitled to our own set of facts." Cast yourself as an honest broker trying to make things better for everyone.

JEREMY

My predecessor, Julianna Smoot, often had to deal with disruptive behavior at the White House. In June 2010, PBS was working on an installment of *In Performance at the White House,* this one honoring Paul McCartney when he was awarded the Library of Congress Gershwin Prize for Popular Song. It promised to be a memorable evening, but it almost didn't happen. Prior to the event, McCartney's representatives requested that his armed bodyguard be allowed into the White House during rehearsals and the performance. The Secret Service denied the request, citing that no armed individuals, other than the Secret Service, could be on the White House property. (After all, there is probably no place on earth more protected.)

Once the request was denied, someone tenacious in McCartney's camp added the bodyguard's name to the "production list" and submitted it to the Secret Service, obviously hoping it would sneak through. The Secret Service was not pleased about the attempt to slip past them and once again refused him access.

McCartney's team insinuated to Cappy McGarr, the show's executive producer, that he wouldn't attend. McGarr quickly called Julianna Smoot. "I would never place a call to Julianna's direct cell phone unless it was an emergency," McGarr said, "and this is."

Smoot contacted Joseph Clancy, who would later become the director of the Secret Service, and asked if there was anything that he could do to help. After they talked it through, Clancy said they would consider allowing the bodyguard into the complex if he agreed to come unarmed and in a civilian capacity, as a guest of the president and first lady. McCartney's team agreed, and the evening was saved. Rather than instigate a showdown, Julianna deflected and managed the situation.

EMOTIONALLY DISENGAGE

We are at our most vulnerable when there's no leverage to be used against an abrasive person, when our repeated efforts to get along with him or her have been exhausted, and there's no one else to ask for help. These extremely trying situations require strong responses. If there is no way to ignore or manage a true incorrigible with whom you must interact every day, don't rule out emotional disengagement. If your boss screams at you in front of your coworkers, accusing you of incompetence and laziness, don't engage. Silence and a noncommittal expression deprive a confrontational person of the drama he needs to keep his anger going.

Try to remain calm and centered while transcending the noise and vitriol of the aggravating person. You don't need to be profoundly enlightened to exercise detachment; consciously take deeper, more regular breaths, and be aware of your body's reaction. Realize that the difficult person must feel very threatened to behave as he does. Consider how he looks to the others present: he may appear to have the upper hand at the moment, but his outburst diminishes him. Remember that being rude is simply an imitation of strength. To blunt the tirade, you can acknowledge you hear what he's saying. Responding "Please don't yell at me" is strong but respectful. And don't leave the room, however much you may want to, until the conversation is over, or your next confrontation with this person will be equally awkward.

Few of us can stand to be belittled, but if you detach yourself emotionally and refuse to engage at the aggressor's level, you create your own zone of safety. Think of yourself as an impenetrable fortress that no assault can breach as long as you don't rush into battle. You can't change another person's behavior, but you can change how you respond to it.

And at the end of a workday, go home and *forget about it*! If you spend your free time obsessing over every unhappy exchange and dirty look your boss gives you, you'll make yourself miserable. Don't give him that power. Go for a workout, spend time with a friend who makes you laugh, see a movie you love—anything that puts your job behind you until the next day. Don't brood and don't wear out your significant other talking about it. This is where perspective comes in: work is a part of life but it should never be your whole life.

WHEN ALL ELSE FAILS,
SAY SOMETHING

As much as we advocate serene detachment, it would be naive to think it always works. There are times when you have to take a stand, not just for the sake of correcting something that's unfair but in order to maintain your own self-respect.

JEREMY

In December 2012, a holiday dinner for loyal supporters provided another test for me. As the dinner was ending, the president got up from his table and began to thank each person individually. At one point, he called me over to a table where he was chatting with the guests. Even if I had tried, I could have never anticipated the president's question—about the candles in the menorah. "Are the candles kosher?" he asked. One of the guests, with whom I had spoken earlier and who could have raised the topic then, had instead told the president directly she thought that they were not—and if so, that would be highly offensive.

My heart started pounding, but I kept the facade of being very calm and didn't let my frozen smile evaporate. I responded that we would confirm that they were kosher and felt certain that Jarrod Bernstein, the director of Jewish outreach in the Office of Public Engagement, would not have missed such a detail.

The president was understandably concerned, and so was I. Then Jarrod reassured me that the candles were indeed kosher. In addition to relaying the information to the president, I informed the guest. Her response was surprising: she retorted that she really didn't think they *weren't* kosher; she just "thought it was a good conversation starter." I politely let the guest know that in her hope to have something "meaningful" to say to the president, she created unnecessary stress. I hope that she will think carefully before asking a needlessly provocative question again.

LEA

Sometimes it's important to say something to head off a potentially disruptive situation. During the 2004 presidential campaign, Lindsay Reynolds, who went on to become the chief of staff to First Lady Melania Trump, was sent to organize a campaign event with Laura Bush at the southern mansion of a significant fundraiser. The host thought the perfect spot for photos with Mrs. Bush would be in their living room in front of the marble fireplace, which was right below a life-size portrait of the host's wife—fully nude and sprawled on a bearskin rug in all her glory. The heads of the guests (and first lady) would have been just beneath the painting. Asking to have the picture removed might have given offense, and the protocol for a political event in a supporter's house is to make it as homey as possible. Thinking quickly, Lindsay told the hosts a new campaign policy required all photos to have a plain blue background, and they didn't argue. Finding an alternative that didn't embarrass the hosts or the guest of honor prevented an awkward situation—and some unthinkable photos—for everyone concerned.

Both of the first ladies we served were subject to criticism from all corners. They made use of all of the possible strategies:

ignoring, staying good-humored, managing and deflecting, and emotionally disengaging from those who attacked them. No one would want to be the focus of such vitriol, yet both women learned to endure and rise above it. "When they go low, we go high" would become a famous line of Michelle Obama's during the 2016 campaign, but it was something both women practiced for many years. It took strength and perspective, and those of us who worked around them benefited from their example.

Michelle Obama said in an interview with Oprah Winfrey at the close of the administration, "There's so much that comes at us all the time, every day, in subtle ways that could tear your soul apart if you let it. . . . You better brush it off." Laura Bush said in 2014 that she watched the first President Bush and his wife, Barbara, endure political ridicule and knew what to expect. "That doesn't make it any less hurtful," she said, "and anyone that's in a leadership position of any sort knows you're going to be criticized, and a target for criticism." Neither of these women let this often-anonymous hatred define them.

Dealing with very difficult people or situations requires patience, resolve, and restraint. While the goal of this book is to encourage and nurture good relationships, we know that this is not always possible. That's why developing strategies for managing the unmanageable is a vital skill to cultivate.

We close with two final observations about difficult people. The battles they seek and the conflict they create aren't really with you but with themselves. Remembering that makes it easier to view them with some level of compassion. And continuing to treat such a person with equanimity, despite the abuse he or she hands out, is a reflection of your own good character and integrity.

CHAPTER 11

Virtual Manners

✧ ✧ ✧

Be civil to all, sociable to many, familiar with few,
friend to one, enemy to none.

Benjamin Franklin

I n the eleven years between Lea's 2004 arrival in the White House and Jeremy's departure in 2015, advances in technology and social media changed a lot about the way we did our jobs. In the Bush administration, invitations and RSVPs were sent through the mail and responses taken on the telephone. Every interaction with a person in the residence required a call or an in-person visit. Most guests had BlackBerries, but few had camera phones. Facebook accounts were for college students, Twitter had barely made a peep, and there was no Instagram, let alone Snapchat. Social media hadn't yet become a source for news or a political tool.

Fast-forward to the Obama years: invitations and RSVPs were managed online, calligraphers made emailable PDFs of invitations (actual invitations were sent or handed out as keepsakes), and nobody would dream of coming to the White House without a smartphone. For guests, recording their visit became almost as important as actually being there.

Neither of us could have been nearly as productive in the Social Office without technological advancements, of course. When we wanted to invite entertainers to perform at the White House, we'd find the right contact information on their website and were able to get their managers on the phone within minutes. When we were expecting important visitors, we'd Google their images so we could welcome them by name. Thanks to smartphones, we could text or email Social Office staff about real-time changes during unfolding events so that everyone pivoted automatically to the new plan: "Head of state and wife arrived for dinner with ambassador in tow. Tell calligraphers need extra menu and place card, and ushers another place setting at the table." Such technology was a godsend.

But while we appreciated our new capabilities, we knew we had to strive to maintain the same level of courtesy online that we did in all of our personal interactions. In our rush to be more productive, most of us are glued to our devices all day, every day, but there isn't much instruction for civilized behavior in emails and texts and on social media platforms. This is all the more reason that we must do our best to use the techniques we've learned so far to prevent miscommunication and the isolation that comes with spending more time online than we do in face-to-face conversations. It takes a conscious effort to treat one another well in the digital realm.

LEA

During my tenure, the seating for events was done on computer software designed by the White House technical support office; we could seat hundred-person dinners in an hour without forgetting anyone or seating them twice, a task that would otherwise have taken all day. I remember poring over the little circles of a seating chart for an important Senate Spouses' Luncheon, tapping names into the program efficiently—or so I thought. Finally, satisfied with the plan, I sent it upstairs to Mrs. Bush, who immediately noticed that I'd seated Lynda Robb and Susan Allen next to each other. Lynda Robb's husband, Democratic Senator Chuck Robb, had lost his Senate seat in a divisive election in 2000 to George Allen. Susan Allen was a current Senate spouse, and Lynda Robb was now a former Senate spouse as a result of that hard-fought race. Mrs. Bush pointed this out, and I quickly rearranged the seating, preventing what could have been a miserable lunch for those two women. It was a lesson in how the personal often trumps the digital.

MIND YOUR PHONE

Phones may have become indispensable, but our relationship with them can veer toward the compulsive. Jeremy once observed the guest of honor at a White House event reading texts on his phone while standing onstage in the East Room and being introduced by President Obama. What a vivid reminder not to let your life pass you by while you're busy looking down at a screen.

LEA

A friend who was fundraising for a presidential campaign was very excited when he managed to get a meeting with a powerful Fortune 500 CEO. The executive was known for his abrupt manner, so my friend planned his presentation carefully, but during the pitch, he couldn't help glancing at his BlackBerry when the CEO was talking. The CEO stopped, pointed to the BlackBerry, and said, "Can I see that?" Thinking that the CEO was interested in his device, he handed it over and enthusiastically began describing its newest features. The CEO took the BlackBerry and silently hurled it across the room, where it hit the wall and broke into pieces. He then resumed the conversation as if nothing had happened.

My rattled friend left with nothing but the remnants of his phone—and a valuable lesson about the arrogance of checking emails in the middle of an important business meeting.

There is a generational element to this story: the older the person you're dealing with is, the more insulted he or she will likely be by the intrusion of technology into a conversation. The millennials among us may think it's okay to check their phones constantly in front of others, but they should remember that they're making an impression, so they might as well make it a good one.

In general, people deserve more attention than phones do. As someone we know likes to say, "The person in person is more important than the person on the phone." Put your device out of sight when you're talking to someone. If you must take an important call, apologize in advance and move to a private area. Unless you're waiting for news of a big deal that everyone is in on, checking your email during meetings is inconsiderate to everyone present. Being visibly tethered to your phone might make you feel important, but it sends a message of disrespect to others and suggests that you lack the willpower to set it aside and focus on the conversation. The same is true as you go about your neighborhood errands. If you're using earbuds and stop to chat with someone, remove them and give the person your full attention. When you buy something at the drugstore, make eye contact with the salesperson instead of checking the latest football scores. As always, remember how it feels when you're on the receiving end of an exchange with someone who barely looks up.

There are things no one should discuss in public on a phone, such as confidential business information or the intimate details of your romantic life. When you're on a train or bus, refrain from describing your racy weekend to your best friend to avoid embarrassing other passengers. Talking freely about pending business deals exposes your strategies to anyone within earshot. Save the scoop, whether personal or professional, for a more discreet setting. Don't shout when you're talking in a public place, and do not put your phone in speaker mode in a doctor's waiting room or other communal area. If you're talking one-on-one and would prefer to use speaker mode, ask the other person's permission first, no matter where the conversation is taking place.

There are a few locations where you should refrain from using your phone. The "never" category includes churches, mosques, and temples; funerals and weddings; and while driving. The "sometimes" category includes theaters, movie houses, or museums, provided you move to the lobby; and the "only when absolutely necessary" categories are in the restroom, at meals with others, or while walking.

When you're at a restaurant or dinner party with friends, don't put your phone on the table or on your lap so you can keep looking at it throughout the meal. If you must take an important call, excuse yourself. The arrival of the check does not signal permission to pull out your phone. Wait until everyone gets up.

We believe in the power and efficiency of a phone call. We find it's better to call when you're letting your boss know that you won't be coming to work, if you have some bad news to share with someone, or when you need to be persuasive. It's much more difficult to say no to a person on the phone than it is to say no in an email or text. If you really want something, pick up that phone and use those skills of confidence, charm, and conflict resolution.

EMAIL ALERTS: ALCOHOL, ANGER, AND AUTOCORRECT

In the ethics briefings that all new White House employees must attend before beginning their jobs, one of the many things discussed is how to use the government email accounts. The ethics lawyers say, "Don't write anything in an email that you wouldn't be comfortable reading on the front page of the *Washington Post*." This is very good advice, especially now that the hacking of emails has become a spectator sport. Any intemperate, inappropriate, mean-spirited thing you write can be forwarded or excerpted anywhere, at any time, so edit yourself accordingly. Forwarding an email you've received can be a real time-saver; just make sure you aren't sharing something confidential or disreputable. It's bad form to forward an email containing personal opinions that were meant for your eyes only.

More and more of our interactions take place over text or email. Without the ability to read another person's facial expressions, body language, and inflections, it's easy to misinterpret a message. When you greet a coworker who's been on vacation with an exuberant smile and say, "Finally! I thought you'd never get back!" you send a very different message from an email that says, "Finally! I thought you'd never get back!" which might read as resentful. Some first and second ladies we have known use a brief but friendly email style that always begins with a warm greeting, gets immediately to the point, and is closed with an affable "Hope all is well" or "Thinking of you" before signing off. First ladies have to keep their emails short out of necessity, both because they're busy and because someone or other is always trying to hack their accounts, which is also why they never write anything that the whole world couldn't read. It's a pretty good approach.

Here are a few tips to make text and email exchanges in the workplace less vulnerable to misinterpretation:

> **Be straightforward.** Sarcasm is difficult to recognize without hearing the speaker's tone of voice or seeing the smile and accompanying eye roll. Save emojis and overpunctuation for your friends. Messages that are all in capitals denote ANGER.

> **Be timely.** Write back quickly, even if it's only to say you can't properly respond at the moment and will be back in touch as soon as possible. Then the sender can't misconstrue your lack of response as disinterest or disrespect. (You can take more time to respond to personal emails.)

> **Be polite.** Identify the reason for your email in the "Subject" line, and if you're emailing someone you don't know, use salutations that are appropriate, such as "Dear Ms. Smith." In business emails, use the same format as you would in writing an actual letter. Avoid abbreviations like "thx" for "thanks" so you don't seem hurried and overly casual. Unless you're in the middle of a real-time email back-and-forth, you should always use some kind of sign-off at the end of the email, such as "All the best" or "Best regards," and your name. Adding a standard signature that includes your name, title, work address, and phone number is helpful for those who may want to follow up.

Don't bring alcohol into the mix. Avoid responding to business questions after you've had a glass or two. Your reply will lack the coherence and consideration that it deserves, and you may need to walk it back the next day.

Don't overreact. When you receive a message that makes you upset, take a moment before answering. Remind yourself: *Emails are forever.* How many of us have blasted off angry responses that were completely out of proportion and lived to regret it? As with handling conflicts, a measured response is better than a rash one. You make more of an impact when you stay calm and marshal your facts logically.

Go easy on "Reply All." Your emails may end up going to people who were not meant to see them or annoy people who don't need to.

Double-check everything. Auto-correct, auto-fill, and auto-reply can be dangerous. To her embarrassment, Lea once sent an attachment of her joint tax return to a Washington insider because his last name was similar to that of her accountant. If you want to be certain you don't send an email too soon, leave the "To" line blank until the very last second; this will prevent you from sending a draft before you've completed your thought process.

Express gratitude. It's fine to send a fulsome thank you via email. It's not as good as a handwritten note, but it's better than not thanking someone at all.

LEA

I once sent an email to a salesman to thank him for helping me find a rug I'd been searching for. He'd made a special effort to locate it, and I wanted to tell him how much I appreciated it. At the end of the email, I wrote, "You're a peach!" Unfortunately, the auto-fill on my computer changed my words to, "You're a douche!" Of course, I didn't notice. I received a call from him a little while later.

"Have I done something to offend you?" he asked.

"No, why?" I replied.

"Maybe you should look at the email you just sent me," he said.

It made me cringe. How can a feature meant to make us more accurate get it so wrong?

TEXT AND SUBTEXT

When texting, it's best to respond quickly and succinctly, use enough punctuation and grammar to be clearly understood, and add your name if you're contacting someone you don't know well. A useful rule of thumb is that if it takes more than three texts to solve a problem, stop texting and pick up the phone.

And we all know this, but we can never say it enough: stay away from emails and texts when you're under the influence of a controlled substance. While an essential "airing of the truth" text to an ex seems like a good idea after a liquid night out, the next morning can feel like a virtual walk of shame, one that never ends if your ex ends up sharing it with others.

If you're texting about a group outing, remove people who can't come from the conversation. They probably aren't interested in every detail of your ongoing debate about where to go for dinner.

Texting a thank you for something minor is fine if it's a very good friend (just make sure it doesn't go on and on). Never text condolences, apologies, or elaborate plans. A "When's the funeral?" text is not appropriate. And refrain from texting information that is confidential or inappropriate.

YOU ARE WHAT YOU TWEET

Once again, knowing when to draw boundaries is vital, and these need to be constantly refined and monitored to keep up with technological and personal evolutions. Just as you want your limits to be adhered to, it's important to respect other people's time, feelings, and privacy.

Twitter, Facebook, Instagram, and Snapchat are meant to be interactive and engaging, so tweet and post with an intent to share useful or entertaining information. Constantly asking for retweets and likes can seem a bit desperate, as does using too many hashtags or posting too many times a day. When others tweet at you, try to respond; this too is a form of relationship building.

JEREMY

I recall a conversation I had with Mrs. Obama when the boom in personal devices had just started. "Who wants to announce to the world where and what they are consuming?" she asked. "Don't people desire privacy?" It is understandable that the first lady, who was so closely watched, coveted privacy, but her questions are worth considering by all of us.

Ubiquitous phones and the prodigious taking of selfies required us to enforce new smartphone policies for certain White House events. As technology became more deeply entrenched in the culture, the first lady thought it was more important for people to enjoy the moment rather than being preoccupied by taking a photo or video. She also wanted everyone's privacy to be respected. Finally, she was aware that posting photos of an event could create hurt feelings for those who weren't invited. For personal events, we implemented a "no social media" rule. Guests were required to check their phones downstairs. They could go down to retrieve messages, but they had to check the phone back in before returning upstairs. There were occasional offenders, but when posts ended up online, the White House became aware of it quickly. People were usually asked to remove the post—and we knew who the culprits were before compiling the guest list for the next event.

Even if your hosts aren't the president and first lady of the United States, be civil and courteous about your social media posting and respect their wishes. Keep in mind that though some of us share almost every detail of our lives on social media, others prefer to limit their online presence or avoid it altogether. It is inappropriate to post wedding pictures of the bride and groom before they have had a chance to do so. They may be just fine with a posting, but always ask first.

Distinguish between work and personal life. Be judicious about what you post, and keep your business and social lives separate. Just as you wouldn't wear a suit to a family picnic, don't be afraid to use different forms of social media for different purposes. If you find you're using your social media for business, create a separate account and keep it professional. Snapchat or Instagram is great for friends, but point colleagues toward LinkedIn. Reserve a closed Facebook account for friends and family and an open one for professional purposes. (That way, if your supervisor wants to friend you, there is a designated place for it.)

But even on your personal Facebook page, don't post photos

that would embarrass you in your work or school environment. Be aware that the face you present to the world online may not be the face you want your boss or your mother to see; just because your page is private doesn't mean there aren't ways for others to access it. One of Lea's friends is a high school football coach. When he noticed that some of his players were coming into practice exhausted and having difficulty remembering the plays, he began looking at their Facebook pages. He found that some of them were partying hard on weekends, and it was affecting their game. He told the boys that they could follow the team rules or leave.

We've all read the news stories of students whose acceptances to Ivy League schools were rescinded after administrators discovered explicit or inappropriate messages on what students mistakenly thought was a private group chat. Social media are hazardous for students and employees alike. Nothing is private. A screen grab can immortalize the most ephemeral post. It doesn't matter if your joke is just for friends or that you're being ironic. Jokes that you see as harmless can easily be misconstrued. Steer clear of offensive material unless you like the idea of it following you around.

JEREMY

I was surprised to learn that numerous job applicants, whom the Social Office interviewed and wanted to hire, did not end up getting a position because the counsel office did not "vet" them thanks to things they had written or posted on Facebook. Michelle Obama told the *Today Show* in 2012 that her daughters were "one of the first kids in the White House growing up where everybody's got a cell phone." She warned her girls that the consequence is that "everybody's watching . . . you can't go off on somebody . . . because you may be having a moment, but somebody could use that moment and try and define you forever. What you put on the Internet, what you say now, can be a part of your life forever."

There will never be sufficient guidelines where Facebook, Instagram, Twitter, Snapchat, and the next new thing are concerned, but here are some basic standards:

Ask first. Get permission before posting photos of friends, their homes, their children, or their parties.

Be kind. Don't put up unflattering photos of others unless you want the same treatment.

Pare down. Clean up your page periodically to get rid of outdated posts. Also adjust your privacy settings to make sure things that are personal to you stay that way.

Don't steal images or ideas. Give credit if you're retweeting or re-gramming someone else's content.

Be discreet. Be mindful when you're in a professional setting. There might be things that don't belong online—blueprints for a building, financial statements, and memoranda about pending legal issues, for example.

Don't post to boast. We know this might sound obvious, but making people envious is not the way to develop friendships or influence people. Unless you're a blogger with something to sell, making people green with envy about what you own, eat, or visit doesn't pay.

Like it or not. Don't obsess about being "liked." You have nothing to prove to anyone. You know who you are and shouldn't need others to validate you.

Not all of us are as digitally adept as the average fifteen-year-old. It's a kindness to offer to help members of the older generation who don't have ready access to the intricacies of online shopping, their grandchildren's school photos, or food blog recipes. Helping others find the right technological tools will open more people to the beneficial aspects of being digitally savvy, so that they can keep up with the times. Similarly, older people should refrain from grousing about how the younger generation is obsessed with their phones. Don't be condescending in either direction—try to reach across the technological divide.

DIALING IT DOWN

We all have to take control of our technology. Discipline yourself not to look at your phone every few minutes; try to stay away for longer and longer stretches. You will become more productive and focused on the job and the people in front of you. If you're working on a big project, avoid the constant distraction of unrelated texts and email. (Auto-reply can be a great tool to let people know you're on deadline.) Let the "do not disturb" setting be your friend, and when you can, physically remove your phone from your sight and go device free for a couple of hours. It's liberating and allows you to treat yourself with the same respect you afford others.

LEA

A truly considerate person is someone who doesn't even appear to own a phone. I didn't see either of the Bushes' cell phones more than twice in two years; they never took them out in public or even with most staff. If you were with them, you had their full attention, and it wasn't just because they had personal aides to look out for them. They wouldn't take a call in front of a visitor. It was a matter of respect that protected their privacy as well as the privacy of others. It's healthy to be in control of your devices rather than allowing them to control you.

Just as we ignore and disengage from disruptive and difficult people in real life, we advocate doing the same online. The anonymity of the Internet makes it easy for people to post offensive things with little consequence, and we need to resist the temptation to be drawn into ugly diatribes that have no place in our personal or national conversations. It's wonderful that online networks bring together people who would otherwise never meet, but always remember that when you're online, you're still talking to a real person with feelings. Like all forms of etiquette, the guidelines we create for using technology should be rooted in common courtesy and respect.

CHAPTER 12

Details Matter

Do the best you can in every task, no matter how
unimportant it may seem at the time. No one learns more
about a problem than the person at the bottom.

SANDRA DAY O'CONNOR

While you might think as you progress through your
career that details should be left to people just starting
out, those who understand true responsibility know that paying
attention is a hallmark of leadership.

Winston Churchill involved himself in every aspect of British life during World War II, from personally investigating cases
of class discrimination in the British armed services to conducting studies into the best diet for enlisted men. (On finding that
life without tea for the British people would be detrimental to
morale, he decided to continue to import tea for as long as possible, despite the cost.) He studied weaponry to such a degree
that he was able to suggest where to place additional pieces of
armor on British tanks to better protect the troops. Nothing was
beneath his attention.

Like loyalty, charm, and humor, noticing and acting on details
is another important way to let others know we value them.

During her tenure as second lady, Dr. Jill Biden's attention to detail was remarkable. Down-to-earth, bright, and unassuming, she always sent considerate notes and whenever she walked into a room, she made a point to acknowledge everyone present. She also remained closely involved in causes that mattered deeply to her such as Community College to Career, support and engagement for military families, and cancer research. As a result, her staff was immensely devoted to her. Jeremy will never forget the fact that on the day he arrived at the White House, she invited him to join a hot-yoga session; on his final day, she penned a thoughtful letter, even as her son Beau was in the hospital, gravely ill.

No detail is unimportant, as Jeremy was reminded one afternoon as he was talking to one of the Secret Service agents near the Visitors Office in the East Wing. Jeremy noticed an empty wheelchair and sat down for a moment to test it out. He was surprised at how narrow it was and wondered how it could ever accommodate some of their larger guests. Imagining the possibility of such a humiliating scenario, he immediately resolved to order larger ones. A few months later, as he was accompanying a guest using the newly acquired chair in the elevator, she commented on what a relief it was that the White House wheelchair wasn't like "those awful petite airline seat–style chairs" that she encounters so often.

Some people do have greater intuition when it comes to zeroing in on the little things that matter, but anyone can learn how to heed the small stuff. We found six ways you can hone your ability to identify important details and make it clear to others that you care: define your day, remember names, personalize parties, say thank you early and often, pay it forward, and acknowledge those behind the scenes.

DEFINE YOUR DAY

Organizing your time, your desk, and your mind-set will maximize productivity and minimize stress. It's much easier to treat people well when you're feeling on top of things. Here are some simple ways to marshal the details of your job and your life:

Get a head start. We used to come to work very early in the morning to have time to sit quietly and form a game plan. The early morning is also a good time to check in with other staff before they get caught up in meetings of their own.

Take notes. We can't emphasize this enough: if you don't write it down, you'll forget most of it as you exit the conference room. Lea carried a 5-by-7-inch spiral notebook with her everywhere and wrote everything down in it. She also kept a notepad at her bedside: she found that those ideas that float up through the subconscious during the night are often the most creative and important.

Keep track of your time. Maintain a daily calendar, either on paper or electronically, that you can update throughout the day as meetings or other appointments are added to your schedule. Being able to see both the calendar and the notes at a glance helps keep the whole picture together.

Organize your files. Whether online or in a file cabinet with manila folders, keep project files and contact information up-to-date and easily accessible. Lea kept upcoming event files, stored chronologically and by name, on top of her desk. (This is especially helpful if you're working on the same kinds of projects again and again—you don't have to start planning from scratch each time.)

When Mrs. Bush called to ask a question about an event, she was able to pull open the file and answer her immediately. Jeremy kept both digital and paper files of each event, arranged by date, in case there was a computer issue. And large, poster-size monthly calendars filled the wall right outside his office—making it easy for everyone to refer to the schedule for the next four months.

Proofread obsessively. Typos matter. One spelling error can make you look sloppy and sink your credibility. For the White House holiday decor booklets, which were given to visitors on tours during the holiday season, Jeremy would send a final draft to his perfectionist Aunt Martha in San Antonio, who worked doing research at the Alamo for years and would note any questionable use of grammar or style. She would inevitably catch a few items, preventing mistakes from making it into the final product.

Be punctual. Estimate how long each element of the day will take, and then stick to your schedule. Putting the day on paper, as we did in our event "line-by-lines," is a long-established tradition in the government that accounts for every minute of the workday and keeps everything running on time. Build in short breaks to release stress and absorb inevitable delays.

Keep meetings essential and brief. Regular staff meetings are important, but don't waste others' time if you don't have anything new to report or discuss. Ask the attendees to be on time. Have an agenda ready, and refer to it throughout your meeting to be certain that everyone has a chance to bring up relevant issues. When you become known as someone whose meetings matter, people will be more likely to show up.

Think ahead. Set aside time each week to strategize about the coming month, quarter, and year, and maintain a list of large projects that are in the offing. Just thinking about them will give you the momentum to get started. And starting a to-do list for the next day allows you to leave work knowing your affairs are in order and you have a jump on tomorrow.

PLAY THE NAME GAME

We loved to greet people by name when they came to the White House and would run through the guest lists before an event to refresh our memories. It proved to be a worthwhile effort, because we came to see how much it meant to others. Being welcomed by name was an extra bit of attention that made people positively preen with delight.

Everyone has found themselves at some point standing in a circle of new people at a party or work event with the host throwing out each person's name and profession like a blackjack dealer flipping cards in a casino. By the time the conversation resumes, you have no idea who anyone is or what he or she does, and it can be hard to make a connection. But a little later, one of those vaguely familiar faces from the circle comes up to you, addresses you by name, and you experience a sudden rush of happiness. Cultivate your powers of attention to detail, and you can be the person who unexpectedly recollects a name at a party and makes a great impression.

Here's a quick lesson from veteran social secretaries on how to remember people's names—a particular challenge for Jeremy. When being introduced to someone for the first time, repeat the name out loud. Take your time, and think of the person's name while you're looking at him or her, mentally fusing the name with the face. Create a mnemonic device, some connection that helps

201

you to recall the name, such as, "Bob, who looks like a bear, is from Chicago—Chicago Bears Bob." It's worth the effort, because you never know when that person might come back into your life again.

And it's not just names. We found that remembering something about a person's likes and dislikes often made all the difference between a person feeling comfortable about attending a White House party or not. The wife of a member of Congress suffered from a fear of crowds. Every time she was able to bring herself to come to the White House, we made a special effort with her, asking about subjects we knew were comfortable for her: her children, her garden, her summer plans. Her husband always thanked us for being so kind to his wife.

PERSONALIZE YOUR PARTIES

Whether it's a black-tie bash or a backyard barbecue, a successful party isn't about the budget; it's about the thought behind it. A formal event that features the most expensive florist in town and a lavish spread can still feel soulless. The more attention you pay to the details, the more warm and memorable the party will be.

If you're planning an event for a boss, the best way is through a large group effort—and here, as always, it's about using details that show you know and care about the person. The Clinton White House staff demonstrated their affection for Hillary Clinton at her birthday celebrations each year. Ann Stock, social secretary to the Clintons for four years, organized the first surprise costume birthday party for Mrs. Clinton in 1993. Ann arranged for the White House lights to be turned off, and Mrs. Clinton was taken up the elevator to her bedroom to find a Dolley Madison costume awaiting her. After changing, she was led down the back steps in darkness, to be surprised in the East Room by costumed friends and staff—and President Clinton, dressed as James Madison.

Another year, Ann organized a sock hop birthday for Mrs. Clinton and had a pink poodle skirt made for the first lady. She got Casey Kasem to DJ, and transformed the party space to look like Hillary Rodham's old living room in Park Ridge, Illinois. Mrs. Clinton was thrilled with the parties, and every element her staff attended to showed how highly she was regarded.

All great hostesses operate on the same theory articulated by Dwight Eisenhower when referring to the D-Day invasion: "Plans are useless, planning is indispensable." The more you anticipate ahead of time, the less you'll have to think about once things get started.

Here are a few pointers that will allow you to pick up a glass and enjoy the party alongside your guests:

Choose a theme. Themes are a great organizing tool: green-and-white cupcakes for your favorite golfer; vodka martinis ("shaken, not stirred") for a diehard James Bond fan; puka shell necklaces and sea salt candles on the tables to celebrate a dedicated surfer. For a wedding anniversary, think of places, stories, and pastimes that will remind guests of the couple's life together and weave those elements into the decor, menu, and party favors.

RSVP requested! However you extend your invitations and however informal the party, ask guests to respond. It's difficult to plan a party when you don't know how many people are coming. If you haven't heard back from someone, it's okay to follow up. You may feel awkward, but it's less embarrassing than running out of food or drinks.

Do ahead. The more details you've taken care of beforehand (stocking up on ice, bringing out extra chairs, creating a playlist on Spotify), the less stressful the party itself will be. Mentally tick through the stages of the event, and make sure you have everything you need, from cocktail napkins to coat hangers. Don't think of a party as an opportunity to test new recipes.

A warm hello. Guests should be greeted by name, promptly introduced to others, and shown where to put coats and handbags. It's nice to offer a festive cocktail created especially for the evening, along with having a tray of water and wine nearby so people can serve themselves. For those who don't drink, provide a batch of interesting "mocktails," such as an alcohol-free mojito or sparkling fresh-fruit lemonade.

What to bring? If guests offer and you're amenable, suggest they bring nonessential items. You don't want to be without a dessert! After-dinner chocolates or wine are always safe suggestions.

For smaller guests. If you're planning an outdoor birthday party for five-year-olds (a good rule of thumb for children's birthday parties: invite the number of children who correspond to the age of the birthday boy or girl to keep things manageable), think about what you might do if it rains. Plan three more activities than you think you'll need, and don't let the party last more than ninety minutes. (We promise it will feel like three hours to you.)

Leave them smiling. As guests depart, give them a small token of the evening. If a party is going to extend into the wee hours, it could be bags of homemade muffins or granola for next morning's breakfast. In a day or two, send an electronic file of the music playlist you used or a selection of party photos.

LEA

Laura Bush made a practice of inviting her staff for lunch in the residence several times a year, always asking me to plan for beautiful centerpieces, White House china, a formal seating arrangement, and calligraphy menu cards, just as we would have done for a head of state.

She also hosted receptions in the family residence for members of Congress and their spouses—several a week—and would give guests the run of the floor, showing them the hidden staircase to the third floor (a discreet way for the residence staff to move between floors without violating the family's privacy) and encouraging them to take photos of themselves in the Lincoln Bedroom and on the Truman Balcony.

One of the most impressive examples of Mrs. Bush's attention to detail was her practice of seeking out events that would bring people to the White House who had been overlooked in the past. And once they arrived, she didn't just want her guests to have a nice time; she wanted them to have the thrill of their lives. In 2006, she invited all the men who had served in her father's battalion in World War II to a Veterans' Day celebration. It took some effort to locate the former soldiers, most of them living in retirement around the country and not expecting a White House invitation, but it was one of the most joyful events we ever hosted.

In 2008, she welcomed her 1964 graduating class from Robert E. Lee High School in Midland, Texas, to a reunion at the White House, along with the classes of Midland High and George Washington Carver High School, both segregated high schools in Midland in 1964. The event was never publicized, but it was one of her quiet ways of bringing the White House experience to as many people as possible.

SAY THANK YOU

When someone has done something thoughtful for you—a gesture that took time and effort—it's important to say thank you. The best way to do that is to write a thank-you note. You might think a note is too small a detail to worry about or an antiquated custom out of an Edith Wharton novel. In fact, it's a crucial component of treating people well. Thank-you notes are a moment of genuine connection and appreciation and something many people treasure as a keepsake. In the rush of modern life, take the time to write one, and to do it well. We both keep a file of the best thank-you notes we've ever received.

Lea sent an old wooden strawberry basket to a friend for her birthday and received a memorable thank-you note, in which her friend told her that the gift had special meaning because she had always spent her childhood birthdays picking strawberries with her mother. Her personal response made Lea feel happy in return.

If thank-you notes are so important, why do we dread writing them? They *can* feel like a chore, but there are two kinds of people in the world: those who express gratitude and those who don't.

Here are the elements we believe distinguish a great thank-you note from a perfunctory one.

Open with a splash. Don't lead with "Thank you for the . . ." Not only is it unimaginative, but it can also leave you struggling for what else to say. First Lady Jacqueline Kennedy always began beautifully. One note to her decorator Richard Keith Langham started out, "What an eye you have—and how lucky I am to be its beneficiary." It's best to write in the same way you speak—without formality. Some examples of opening lines:

"You are so kind to think of me at Christmas!"

"I cannot tell you how much I appreciated the beautiful [fill in the blank]."

"Last night was the most fun I've had in forever. What an amazing evening!"

Show enthusiasm. After the opening, include a line or two describing why you liked the gift or the party's theme. Then make reference to the thoughtfulness of the individual or her cleverness in coming up with it. If you have an anecdote, this is the place to share it—for example: "I wore the tie twice last week and I'm wearing it as I write," or "I may never forget the sight of that enormous flaming cherries jubilee as you brought it out of the kitchen. It was the most spectacular way to end an unforgettable meal."

End thoughtfully. Saying that you hope to see your benefactor soon is a friendly touch; it shows that you enjoy his or her company. And *now* say thank you. Always use a closing phrase that has some warmth or meaning, such as "Fondly" or "Warmest regards."

Just write it. The most important thing about a thank-you note is to send it. Not sending one creates an uncomfortable situation for the gift giver. It forces her into the awkward position of trying to find out if you *did* get the gift, without appearing to be fishing for a thank you.

A note says it best. There are times when we want to express our gratitude to our mentors or bosses, but this can be tricky; no

207

one wants to look as if he's trying to ingratiate himself with a superior. A letter allows you to say what you feel without others questioning your motives. It requires nothing from the recipient. When a more public thank you needs to be given, follow the advice FDR once offered his son James, who was about to give a speech, "Be sincere, be brief, be seated."

JEREMY

I learned the importance of writing thank-you notes first from my grandmother (though I'm not sure that really took) and then from David Mixner. As soon as we got back to the office after an event, he would sit at his desk and write his thank yous. He instilled in me how important it was to do right away. (If you write the note immediately, the experience is fresh in your mind, and it's done. The longer you wait, the more likely you are to forget to do it.)

By the time I got to the White House, I had become accustomed to sending notes. Furnished with an inexhaustible supply of Crane White House note cards—one of the perks given to senior staff—I wrote notes like it was going out of style (the office supplier commented on how often I placed a reorder).

I also understood their importance from my experience on the receiving end. One letter I'll always cherish was the handwritten note from Laura Bush after her husband's portrait unveiling. The Obamas hosted a lunch for the Bush family before the ceremony and reception. Mrs. Bush made note of every detail: that we had used her upstairs White House china, that we served enchiladas (one of President Bush's favorite dishes), and, especially, how welcome the family felt. Her kind words meant so much.

Heartwarming and memorable notes came from the not-so-famous as well. The ones I received from volunteers who worked on holiday decor were so touching, as were the letters from schoolkids who had attended an event at the White House. It was a great reminder of how lucky I was to be working there and a wonderful distraction from the hectic pace of the job.

PAY IT FORWARD

Observing a situation and then improving it with the application of a few apt details, with no anticipated reward, is a form of thoughtfulness that's long remembered.

Random acts of kindness delight the recipient because they are unexpected. Lea's husband once ran into an elderly friend who was flustered trying to hail a cab during an autumn downpour. Wayne called an Uber and put him into it. Now, every time the man sees Wayne, he never fails to thank him for his help that day.

When you see your office mate buried in her cubicle, up to her ears in work, offering to pick her up lunch or a coffee might be just the lift she needs to keep going. If you're sitting next to a person on a plane who is being very chatty (probably because he's nervous), don't put your earbuds in and ignore him. Spend five minutes listening to how he is on his way to see his relatives. These are the exchanges that define us as human beings.

LEA

One night, I came out to the East Executive parking lot after an all-day snowstorm to find that someone had dug my car out of the snow and scraped the ice off the windows. I had been dreading cleaning off the car, dressed as I was in high heels and a skirt.

I never knew who did it, but I was so grateful that I stopped right there in the snow and started to cry. Any time we do something random and kind, we become instruments of the good. These small acts bring out the best version of yourself.

Everyone can do something considerate for another person, and it doesn't have to be lavish. When George W. Bush hosted heads of state at his ranch in Crawford, he often invited the White House butlers on duty at the ranch to go fishing with him after the dignitaries left, an experience they still talk about with great fondness. It was a thoughtful act, not requiring anything more than his desire to do something nice. And it's just that simple: think about what someone would really appreciate that is within your ability to do, and then do it.

JEREMY

When a Secret Service agent who was a zealous football fan was departing his assignment with the first family (they are always on rotation), Mrs. Obama, after saying a few words of gratitude for his work in ensuring their family's safety, handed him an envelope with two tickets to the SuperBowl.

Just before the state dinner honoring Prime Minister David Cameron and his wife, I was walking with Mrs. Obama on the South Drive, discussing china—something that two years earlier I couldn't have imagined discussing with anyone, much less the first lady. I mentioned how much I loved the Reagan china and how ironic it was because I had grown up in a "non–Reagan loving" family. (I told Gahl Hodges Burt, one of the social secretaries for the Reagans, when we made use of the china, and she told me how much Mrs. Reagan loved hearing it.)

Mrs. Obama laughed and said she also grew up in a similar family but had a new appreciation for Nancy Reagan and the respectful manner with which she had handled the role of first lady. I told Mrs. Obama that Gahl had mentioned to me that Mrs. Reagan had recently broken a rib and was having a difficult recovery. Mrs. Obama asked me for her address and penned a get-well note that day. Several weeks later I received a call from Gahl, who told me how touched Mrs. Reagan was by it.

ACKNOWLEDGE THOSE BEHIND THE SCENES

In work as in the rest of life, there are people whom we tend to take for granted because their actions are so reliable that it's easy to stop noticing them. Official recognition of employees' investments of time and energy is a detail that should not be forgotten: it keeps spirits up, and sets the tone for the day. The Obamas' White House chief of staff, Denis McDonough, always made a point of thanking people in the morning staff meetings—every morning. That positive reinforcement gave staffers the extra surge of energy that they needed to keep up with the demands of the White House.

It would change our entire outlook to come into the office the morning after a particularly frenetic day and find a note from our respective first ladies, thanking us for our efforts. Fatigue and frustration would drain away in a moment; that thoughtful detail made us feel as though what we were doing was important.

JEREMY

At my first holiday senior staff dinner in 2011, I was walking around the State Dining Room to make sure everything was going well. This dinner was a holiday gift from the Obamas to the senior staff for all the work we'd done that year, an especially considerate gesture since we were in the second week of the holidays, and Team Social was running on adrenaline alone. After a performance by K. D. Lang, Mrs. Obama spoke, thanking everyone for their dedication. Then, just before handing the microphone to the president, she said, "And thank you, Jeremy. The White House has never looked so beautiful. And the humor and joy you have brought to the office and to this house is so contagious. Thank you, Jeremy. We love you."

The president also thanked me and I simply nodded my head. I was overwhelmed as applause filled the room. It didn't take much time or energy for Mrs. Obama to acknowledge me—perhaps twenty seconds—but it affected me profoundly. The power of the statement was also heightened by the surprise; I hadn't been expecting it at all.

LEA

President and Mrs. Bush made a regular practice of hosting farewell dinners in their private quarters for staff who had come to the end of their White House service. When I left, they hosted a dinner (the one where President Bush bonded with my daughter over her failing math) and invited me to bring my family and other guests. When I arrived at the White House that night, I was touched to find an honor guard of military social aides waiting for me. They presented me with a drawing of the White

House, which they had all signed, and I was given a formal military escort through the White House to the dinner in the Yellow Oval Room. The honor guard and farewell ceremony were practices I had never seen before, and I was deeply moved. I arrived at the private quarters in tears, where the Bushes waited to greet me.

Attending to the details is something you can do every day—and do well. It will change how others think of you, but it will also make a transformative difference in how you see yourself. Small details are the ones that make a big impact.

CONCLUSION

✧ ✧ ✧

One person can make a difference,
and everyone should try.

John F. Kennedy

A mong our favorite things about our tenures in the White House was seeing the extravagant presents regularly bestowed on the president and first lady. There was a constant flow of heartfelt gifts from ardent constituents: Lea remembers that Dick Cheney received a larger-than-life portrait of himself made from pieces of beer cans, and Jeremy recalls one enthusiastic fan who made a painting of Barack Obama as Jesus Christ, steering a ship in a storm.

Then there were gifts from dignitaries, a long tradition in the White House, from the alligator John Adams received from the marquis de Lafayette to the rug that the Azerbaijani delegation gave Bill and Hillary Clinton with their images woven into the center. When President Suharto of Indonesia presented George H. W. Bush with a nine-foot-long, flesh-eating Komodo dragon during a state visit in 1990, the president expressed his gratitude and excitement in a way that might have surprised some people. But he knew that the dragon was one of the largest in Indonesia and a national treasure, given to show the high esteem in which they held Bush. (The dragon was eventually donated to the Cincinnati Zoo, where it went on to father thirty-two more Komodo dragons—the very definition of a gift that keeps on giving.)

Lea will never forget when Japanese Prime Minister Junichiro Koizumi visited President Bush in 2006 and brought with him a shiny, high-tech collapsible bicycle to give to the president. An avid mountain biker, the president was delighted, and to show it, he unfolded and climbed on the bike, and began to ride it down the red-carpeted hallway of the State Floor. The bicycle was too small for him, and the president zigzagged back and forth precariously, bearing down on the corner that Lea was backed into at the time, narrowly avoiding running into her as he turned the bike away at the last moment. She'll never forget the look on his face as he teetered closer—so full of mischief and fun and totally in control.

The greatest gift we received in the White House, of course, is the one that we wanted to share with you: the gift of treating people well. We consider our former bosses, the Bushes and the Obamas, to be our friends, and we enjoy the times we have together. We also treasure our continuing friendships with the other former White House social secretaries. Truly, we all developed "the hide of a rhinoceros, great endurance and a sense of humor," as Grace Coolidge's social secretary, Mary Randolph, so memorably described it. We've become a closely knit group that gathers several times a year for gossip, reminiscing, and the sharing of raucous inside jokes. All of these women know how to treat those around them with kindness and respect, and our lives are enhanced for knowing them.

The basis for every behavior we've discussed requires each of us to begin with an open-minded attitude. You don't have to sail through life with the joie de vivre of a Disney forest creature, but you won't experience positive outcomes if what you're putting into the world is negative. Fear and anger circumscribe our actions, affect how others perceive us, and diminish our ability to change the things we don't like in our lives. Abe Lincoln said that "most folks are as happy as they make up their minds to be." If you're optimistic enough to accept that treating people with kindness and respect will make them likely to do the same, then you're already on the right path.

There is real power in civility because it's about so much more than etiquette. When you've mastered these skills, you can go forth like a superhero and be a force for good in the world.

LEA

I received a letter several years ago from a young woman who had been one of the RSVP assistants in the Social Office. She wrote to say how much she'd learned by watching how the Social Office staff treated guests. She told me she hadn't understood what she was learning at the time, but now that she'd been out in the world in several different office settings in London and New York, she recognized what a valuable experience the Social Office had been and thanked me for the work ethic she developed at the White House. It was a generous gesture that made me feel as though I'd accomplished something more than putting on a lot of nice parties. I didn't think of myself as someone who could have an effect on another person's life, but that note showed me that I had, and in a good way. It was deeply rewarding.

I'm grateful to the many people who taught me important things: relatives, teachers, colleagues, bosses, and friends. How much smaller my life would have been without them. The time I spent working for Lynne Cheney and Laura Bush changed me; it made me more resourceful, confident, and patient. Most of all, it made me a better person.

JEREMY

I have always been very thankful for the experience of being the White House social secretary, but in 2014, I found that the long hours were taking a toll, as was the disconnect from family and friends who were far away. I had completed my fourth year as social secretary, had been with the administration since the campaign, and there were two years left of Obama's second term. But I was ready for a change.

In January 2015, I decided that it was time for me to leave. I felt I owed the Obamas the respect of hearing it from me first, so I held off on looking at other opportunities despite my discomfort in knowing that I might be jobless for a time. Ironically, I found the lead-up to this conversation much more stressful than the waiting period before my interview years before. I was concerned that Mrs. Obama would feel I was deserting them.

We met in her office, where I had interviewed for the job and attended so many meetings. I started off by saying, "My parents always taught me not to overstay my welcome." Once I told her that I was leaving, she was very reassuring, saying, "You always have a job here while we are in the White House. You are family." I breathed a sigh of relief, and then we talked more as friends than as employee and boss. I explained that I didn't have a job lined up and hadn't discussed my decision with others. She told me about the family's plans and life after the White House. It was an emotional conversation. We hugged and walked out of the office together and down the East Wing hall. Then we parted, and I went to my office to inform my staff. Their tearful reactions were both difficult and comforting.

The next day I ran into the president as he was leaving a meeting in the Map Room. He put his hand on my shoulder and said, "I understand you're abandoning us." He gave me his famous half hug, said he understood that I wasn't "getting rich" working for them, and reaffirmed what FLOTUS had stated—that I was family. When we got to the Oval Office, the president asked me what he could do and whom he could call on my behalf. "I'm serious," he said. "I don't offer that often. But do it while I'm still president. Folks will take the call quicker while I'm working here." It took all of my discipline not to break down crying. It was an extraordinary thing to feel so appreciated.

Happiness tends to be wrapped up in our connection to the rest of the world. You don't need to be rich, beautiful, or famous to be happy. But we have found that you do need to be connected to whatever gives your life meaning, and that usually involves interacting with other people in a fulfilling way.

There's also a wonderful circular quality to treating people well. It's the rising tide of respect and well-being that raises all boats and over time makes the world a better place. The character traits we write about have been venerated for thousands of years in many cultures; the twenty-first century just needs a refresher course in the importance of these universal values.

The White House is a melting pot of different cultures, and it offered us the powerful lesson that the first step to moving smoothly through the world is to realize that we don't all see things from the same perspective. As we encountered different backgrounds, religions, and customs, we needed to be able to adjust our expectations and behavior without giving up our own identities. Whether at a reception for Asian and Pacific Islanders, or the Iftar dinner at the breaking of the Ramadan fast, the White House makes its guests comfortable by honoring their traditions, introducing unfamiliar cultures to the American public, and placing the White House mantle of acceptance over a dazzling variety of customs. It's a fine example of an American ideal: you can respect and honor another's perspective without subscribing to it. That's the essence of civility and freedom.

ACKNOWLEDGMENTS

W ithout the experience we gained working in the White House, this book could not exist. We are deeply grateful to First Ladies Laura Bush and Michelle Obama for all they taught us, both directly and by their example; for their continued efforts to make the world a better place; and for their friendship and counsel. We are honored to have served Presidents Barack Obama and George W. Bush and will never forget their generosity of spirit and encouragement.

A special thanks to our friend and respected journalist Roxanne Roberts, who was the first to suggest we collaborate on a book, and to our agent, Todd Shuster, whose easy confidence and formidable experience made our foray into the publishing world smooth and productive.

There are others who helped us with endless edits and good advice, and we can never sufficiently thank Nan Graham, Kara Watson, and Valerie Steiker at Scribner. We are also deeply appreciative of the efforts of Jancee Dunn, Shannon O'Neill, Andrew Young, and Elias Altman in keeping us moving through the writing process and to Kate Lloyd, Roz Lippel, Ashley Gilliam, Jaya Miceli, Sally Howe, and Emily Greenwald for their support of the publication. Thanks also to Adam Weissler for his research.

We thank Cris Comerford, Bill Yosses, Susan Morrison, Daniel Shanks, Buddy Carter, Ron Guy, and Max Doebler, as well as the Secret Service and East Wing staffs with whom we served.

And finally, to our colleagues, the former White House social secretaries: Deesha Dyer, Julianna Smoot, Desirée Rogers, Amy Zantzinger, Catherine Fenton, Capricia Marshall, Ann Stock, Laurie Firestone, Linda Faulkner, Gahl Hodges Burt, Muffie Brandon, Maria Downs, Lucy Breathitt, Bess Abell, and Letitia Baldrige. The stories you shared with such generosity live on in this book and so, by example, do your endless examples of courtesy, discretion, and strength. You are the true exemplars of treating people well.

Jeremy thanks Gerald Pinciss and Lewis Falb, Jane and Marc Nathanson, Courtney Chapin and Pete Rouse, Fred Hochberg and Tom Healy, Mark Gibson, David Wildman, Steve Nuskiewicz, Richard Jacobs, David Mixner, Esther Murgia, John Gaylord, Cappy McGarr, Philip Greenberg, Bill Carrick, Bill Huggins, Tammy Haddad, Constance Milstein, Pete Souza, Bill Harden, Jonathan Van Meter, Brian Rafanelli and Mark Walsh, and Steve Tyler and Martha Utterback. Also, a special debt of gratitude goes to those in the Social Office who kept me on track and on time, especially Ximena Gonzalez, Stacy Koo, Pantea Faed, Natalie Bookey-Baker, and Klevis Xharda. And thanks to my beloved rescue beagle, Garbo, who was at my side throughout the process.

Lea thanks Liddy and Alice Berman, Missy DeCamp, Anne Stewart, Jessica Lightburn, Caroline Huddleston Haley, and the East Wing staff with whom she served, and Eric Draper. Also thanks to Claire Faulkner, Amy Allman Dean, Lindsay Reynolds, Ron Kaufman, Cathy Hargraves, Tom DeFrank, and Brian Cossiboom at the George W. Bush Presidential Center.

NOTES

INTRODUCTION

xi. *White House Secretary should combine*: White House Historical Association, "The White House Social Secretary," retrieved from https://www.whitehousehistory.org/the-white-house-social-secretary.

1. BEGIN WITH CONFIDENCE

22. *"I'm a Ford"* "Remarks of Gerald R. Ford After Taking the Oath of Office as Vice President." Gerald R. Ford Presidential Library & Museum, December 6, 1973, retrieved September 12, 2016, from http://www.ford.utexas.edu/library/speeches/731206.htm.

22. *Walters was mortified* Gary Walters, transcript of an oral history conducted November 14, 2009, by Richard Norton Smith, Gerald R. Ford Oral History Project, 19–20. https://geraldrfordfoundation.org/centennial/oralhistory/gary-walters/.

2. HUMOR AND CHARM, THE GREAT EQUALIZERS

23. *"A Sense of humor"* "Dwight D. Eisenhower Quotes," retrieved September 22, 2016, from http://www.quotes.net/quote/289.

25. *"Quite all right, Your Majesty"* James Humes, *The Wit and Wisdom of Ronald Reagan* (Washington, D.C.: Regnery Publishing, 2007), 150.

25. *"My esteem in this country"* Jimmy Carter, "Baltimore, Maryland, Remarks at a Fundraising Dinner for Harry Hughes," American

Presidency Project, October 10, 1978, http://www.presidency.ucsb
.edu/ws/?pid=30008.

26. *"If I am uglier"* Saul Sigelschiffer, *The American Conscience: The Drama of the Lincoln-Douglas Debates* (New York: Horizon Press, 1973), 144.

36. *"He had the rare gift"* Edward Wagenknecht, *The Seven Worlds of Theodore Roosevelt* (New York: Lyons Press, 2010), 126.

36. *"I fairly fell in love"* Ibid., 127.

36. *"You can't resist"* Ibid.

3. THE QUIET STRENGTH OF CONSISTENCY

52. *"Your mother was my helpmate."* Julie Nixon Eisenhower, *Pat Nixon: The Untold Story* (New York: Simon & Schuster, 1986), 162.

70. *The house was featured.* Lynne Cheney, "This Is Where Many Vice Presidents Have Lived," *Architectural Digest,* December 2001, http://architecturaldigest.com/story/dick-and-lynne-cheneys-historic -washington-dc-house.

4. LISTEN FIRST, TALK LATER

77. *"I learned that everyone"* Bill Clinton, *My Life* (New York: Knopf, 2004), 19.

87. *"elevates the sensibilities"* Peter Wehner, "Friendship in the Age of Trump," *New York Times,* April 23, 2016, http://www .nytimes.com/2016/04/24/opinion/campaign-stops/friendship-in -the-age-of-trump.html?_r=0.

5. RADIATE CALM

90. *As a sixteen-year-old* Richard Brookhiser, *The Rules of Civility: The 110 Precepts That Guided Our First President in War and Peace* (Charlottesville: University of Virginia Press, 2003).

92. *"Laura is the calm"* Natalie Gott, "First Lady to Champion Literacy, Early Education, Arts," Associated Press, December 16, 2000.

105. *"You decide"* Evan Thomas, *Ike's Bluff: President Eisenhower's Secret Battle to Save the World* (New York: Little, Brown, 2012), 24.

6. HANDLE CONFLICT DIPLOMATICALLY

110. *"What would I do?"* Kenneth T. Walsh, "Bringing Down the Walls, 25 Years Later," *U.S. News and World Report*, November 7, 2014.

7. HONESTY IS THE BEST POLICY
(EXCEPT WHEN IT ISN'T)

123. *"1) He is honest."* H. Paul Jeffers, *An Honest President: The Life and Presidencies of Grover Cleveland* (New York: Harper Perennial, 2002), 368.

9. OWN YOUR MISTAKES

151. *"Embrace every failure"* Jeff Haden, "7 Inspiring Steve Jobs Quotes That Just Might Change Your Life," Inc.com, March 19, 2015, http://www.inc.com/jeff-haden/7-inspirational-steve-jobs-quotes -that-will-change-your-life.html.

165. *Some time later, Maria* Monica Hesse, "Dinner at America's Table: How a White House Rite Evolved," *Washington Post*, October 12, 2011, https://www.washingtonpost.com/lifestyle/style/dinner-at -americas-table-how-a-white-house-rite-evolved/2011/10/11 /gIQAlVZDgL_story.html?utm_term=.0ab527229d8a.

10. KEEP SMILING, AND OTHER WAYS TO DEAL WITH
DIFFICULT PEOPLE

168. *A study of public service* Victor Lipman, "People Leave Managers, Not Companies," Forbes.com, August 4, 2015, http://www.forbes.com /sites/victorlipman/2015/08/04/people-leave-managers-not-com panies/#2bcad39216f3.

168. *When you consider that 46 percent* Dan Schawbel, "Hire for Attitude," Forbes.com, January 23, 2012, http://www.forbes.com/sites/dan schawbel/2012/01/23/89-of-new-hires-fail-because-of-their-atti tude/#15e0f6ac6742.

174. *"We are all entitled"* Steven Weisman, ed., *Daniel Patrick Moynihan: A Portrait in Letters of an American Visionary* (New York: PublicAffairs, 2010).

179. *"There's so much that"* Peter Baker, "2 First Ladies Share Tales of Budding Partnership and Life in the Spotlight," *New York Times*, August 6, 2014, https://www.nytimes.com/2014/08/07/us/politics /2-first-ladies-michelle-obama-laura-bush-share-tales-of-budding -partnership-and-life-in-the-spotlight.html.